ATLANTA
Women Speak

SPEECHES ON IMPORTANT ISSUES
BY PROMINENT ATLANTA WOMEN

Edited by Em Mosier

with assistance from Jim Barber

Foreword by The Honorable Shirley Franklin, Mayor of Atlanta

SB
P

St. Barth lemy Press
Atlanta, GA 30341
www.saintbartsbooks.com

Atlanta Women Speak
Copyright ' 2002 by the YWCA of Greater Atlanta and the Atlanta-Fulton County League of Women Voters.

All rights reserved. Without limiting the rights under copyright reserved above, no part of this publication may be reproduced, stored in or introduced into a retrieval system, or transmitted, in any form or by any means (electronic, mechanical, photocopying, recording, or otherwise), without the prior written permission of the publisher. For information, contact St. Barth lemy Press, 2971 Flowers Rd., South, Suite 100, Atlanta, GA 30341.

This book is available for educational, business or sales promotional use. For information, contact St. Barth lemy Press, 1-800-451-1923.

All speeches were edited according to the Associated Press style. The editor and publisher have used their best efforts to ensure the accuracy of the information in this book. They make no warranty of any kind, express or implied, regarding the information herein.

Printed in the United States of America
Designed by Leigh Skole

ISBN: 1-887617-10-8
Library of Congress Cataloging-in-Publication Data
Available on request

FIRST EDITION
HB Printing 10 9 8 7 6 5 4 3 2 1

For Justine

The rainmaker without whose vision and determination this book would not exist,

And to Mom and Dad

without whose love I would not exist.

m

Table of Contents

FOREWORD IX

PREFACE X

ACKNOWLEDGEMENTS XII

BUILDING BRIDGES IN THE 21ST CENTURY: BETWEEN RICH AND POOR
Joanna Adams to the congregation of Trinity Presbyterian Church 2

THE BUSINESS OF GIVING
Judy Anderson to the Southern Council of Foundations 8

OF SUITCASES AND CANDLES
Kathy Ashe to the Trinity School 6th Grade Graduation 14

MAKING A DIFFERENCE NO MATTER WHERE WE SERVE
Jackie Barrett to the Possible Woman® Leadership Conference 18

AN AFFIRMATIVE-ACTION POSTER PROFESSOR
Linda Bell to the Southern Humanities Council Conference on Justice 22

THE UNQUENCHABLE FIRE
Juel Pate Borders-Benson to the Candler School of Theology, Emory University 30

THE CRISIS IN HOMELESSNESS
Nancy Boxill to the U.S. Congress Select Committee 34

TAX RELIEF FOR SENIOR CITIZENS
Ella Mae Brayboy to the Fulton County Board of Commissioners 38

INDIVIDUAL RESPONSIBILITY
Anna Cablik to the Leadership Atlanta Class 40

LEADERSHIP AT ITS BEST
Pin Pin Chau to the Priority Associates Luncheon 44

DREAMING OF CAMPFIRES
Pearl Cleage to the Women's Resource Center Luncheon 50

CELEBRATING THE ACCOMPLISHMENTS OF WOMEN
Brenda Cole to the Charleston Institute Chapter of Links Inc.,
Women's History Month Program 56

WOMEN IN THE NEW CENTURY: A CALL TO LEADERSHIP
Johnnetta B. Cole to the faculty, students and friends of Mills College 62

WHAT DO MEN KNOW ABOUT TECHNOLOGY THAT WOMEN DON'T?
Chris Coleman to the WebGRRLS/eBusiness Expo 68

BRIDGING THE GAP IN THE CRIMINAL JUSTICE SYSTEM
Betty Ann Cook to the congregation of the Allen Temple AME Church 72

WOMEN AS ENTREPRENEURS
Cathy Cox to the Georgia Women's Entrepreneurs Conference (GWEN) 78

TEACH THE WORDS
Emma I. Darnell to the National CME Annual Convocation 84

TAKE CARE OF THE TULIPS
Stacey Davis to Trinity College, Commencement Address 88

ECONOMIC JUSTICE FOR WOMEN
Stephanie Davis to Women in Finance and Women in Media and Technology 92

WORK-FORCE PREPARATION
Sadie Jo Dennard to the faculty, students and parents at Atlanta Area Tech 96

CHARACTERISTICS WHICH LEAD TO SUCCESS
Nellie Duke to the "Wise Women Speak" Conference 102

BEING THERE
Gail Evans to the Atlanta Women's Foundation 106

. . . A LITTLE BIT ABOUT GIRLS
Jane Fonda to the YWCA of Greater Atlanta's Women of Achievement Luncheon ...110

DIVERSE COMMUNITIES OF HOPE
Renée Lewis Glover to the Atlanta Action Forum 114

LATINOS HAVE EARNED RESPECT FROM GEORGIA
Sara J. González to the Legislative Session, University of Georgia 120

THE LONG VIEW
Beverly Hall to the Atlanta Foundation Forum 124

WOMEN & POWER: CHOOSING TO LEAD
Anne Harper to Spelman College students, faculty and guests 130

IS THERE ANYTHING TOO HARD FOR GOD?
Nina R. Hickson to the congregation of Ben Hill United Methodist Church 136

TABLE OF CONTENTS

THE SECOND TRINITY: GOD, FAMILY & FRIENDS
*Patsy Jo Hilliard to the Divine Unity Missionary Baptist Church,
Family & Friends Day* *140*

THESE THREE: STAND BOLDLY, WALK HUMBLY AND FORGIVE
Alene Isaac to the congregation of Antioch Baptist Church *144*

THE CARE OF A COMMUNITY
Ingrid Saunders Jones to the Sandy Springs Society *150*

LIVING THE DREAMS OF OUR ANCESTORS
*Monica Kaufman to the Grand Marshal's Luncheon,
Mobile Mardi Gras Association* *156*

BRIDGES, NOT BARRIERS
Patricia Russell-McCloud to the National Association of Black Meeting Planners ..*162*

DO YOU SEE WHAT I SEE?
*Cynthia A. McKinney to the MLK Jr. Commemoration Service,
Ebenezer Baptist Church* *168*

THE ROAD TO JUSTICE: THE AFRICAN-AMERICAN LAWYER IN THE FOREFRONT
*Thelma Wyatt Cummings Moore to the Auburn Avenue Research Library,
Annie McPheeters Lecture* *172*

EMBRACING A NEW VISION IN THE 21ST CENTURY
Brenda J. Muhammad to the Butler Street YMCA's Hungry Club Forum *178*

THE IMPORTANCE OF NATURAL HISTORY
Susan Neugent to the Southeastern Council of Foundations *182*

BEING AN ENTREPRENEUR IN ATLANTA
Jenny Pruitt to the Sandy Springs Rotary Club *186*

EVERYBODY WANTS TO GO TO HEAVEN, BUT NOBODY WANTS TO DIE
Catherine L. Ross to the Regional Leadership Institute *190*

SURVIVING DOMESTIC VIOLENCE
Shelley Serdahely to the Women's Resource Center Annual Luncheon *194*

MUSINGS ON THE ARTS
Debbie Shelton to the Alliance Theatre Company Board of Directors *198*

A MEANINGFUL LIFE
Alana Shepherd to the Westminister School Graduation *202*

INVITING SUCCESS
Betty Siegel to Salt Lake Community College, Fall Convocation Address 206

PERSEVERANCE
Cathy Spraetz to the Georgia Executive Women's Network .212

WHAT DOES LEADERSHIP MEAN TO YOU?
Karen Elaine Webster to the Leadership Athens Graduation 216

MARTA'S COMMITMENT TO THE COMMUNITY
Alice T. Wiggins to the International Travel Association 222

BECOMING THE POSSIBLE WOMAN
Linda Wind to the American Association for Women CPAs .228

THE VALUE OF THE VOTE
Judy Woodruff to the Atlanta-Fulton County League of Women Voters 232

EDITORIAL BOARD *238*

SPONSORS *239*

Foreword

Atlanta women speak. They speak each and every day, their voices giving definition to who they are and what they believe. You can hear them all around you – if you listen. Voices ringing out in enthusiastic support of the people and ideals in which they believe; voices that are hushed and soothing, as they bring comfort to those they love; voices that teach, voices that defend, voices that inspire; voices that are loud and strong, as they cry out against injustice; voices that weep over hurt and loss and pain; and voices that are raised in hope, praise and gratitude for the joys and blessings of life. Yes, Atlanta women do speak.

It is my great honor and privilege to have been elected the first female mayor of the great city of Atlanta, especially at the same time Cathy Woolard was elected the first female president of the Atlanta City Council. I am extremely proud of our community, and I call on all who live here to work with us to make Atlanta an even better place for all our citizens. Nonprofit organizations such as the YWCA and League of Women Voters work toward this vision every day, and for these and other fine, charitable organizations, our city is truly grateful.

As you read the wisdom, humor and insights contained in the following speeches, I hope that you will find encouragement, challenge and inspiration. And most of all, I hope it will help you find your own voice.

Shirley Franklin
Mayor of Atlanta

Preface

The League of Women Voters of Atlanta-Fulton County and the YWCA of Greater Atlanta are proud to partner in creating this inspiring publication that comprises a unique collection of speeches by some of Atlanta's most prominent women.

We believe that a publication of this kind is long overdue. These women, who are diverse in ethnicity, cultural values and career paths, have a powerful message for us all. This is not only a compilation of speeches by extraordinary women, but also a celebration of voices that speak to the heart and soul of this great city and nation.

To scholars and critics, this work could justifiably be considered an historical enlightenment and a significant contribution to Atlanta. It is a tribute to the roles women have played in blazing the trail for change and addressing society's most challenging issues. This book also recognizes women who are carrying the torch that provides the light of inspiration and hope for the next generation.

Readers will be deeply touched by Ella Mae Brayboy's tenacity in property tax relief for the elderly. Noted author Pearl Cleage will captivate people with her scathing rendition of child prostitution on Metropolitan Parkway. Jane Fonda will inspire you with her thoughts about the role of women and children in our society. Many will relate to the strong spiritual overtones that make up the essence of who these women really are, and all will connect with the unique blend of fortitude, integrity and compassion that these messages convey.

Above any political party influence, the League of Women Voters, born of the Women's Suffrage Movement, has been committed to voter's registration, education and responsible government. These are important elements to inform and turn citizens into equal, yet active, participants in the success of our great democracy. In 1920, the League won women the right to vote and, some 80 years later, continues its mission to complete the unfinished business of having an equal and inclusive society. For additional information about the League, please call 404-577-8683 or visit the Web site, www.lwvga.org/fulton/.

Founded on the campus of Spelman College in 1902, the YWCA of Greater Atlanta has always been out front, pioneering and transforming the lives of women, girls and their families. Whether delivering quality, affordable learning programs for little ones, preparing homeless women and their families for self-sufficiency or providing guidance for teens to

PREFACE

help them make positive life choices, the YWCA has been a source of strength and a voice for women for over a century. For additional information about the YWCA of Greater Atlanta, please call 404-527-7575, or visit the Web site, www.ywcaatlanta.org.

The collaboration to produce this work was inspired by the similar missions of the League of Women Voters and the YWCA of Greater Atlanta. As leading voices supporting issues most important to women, both organizations agreed that a book of this nature would be educational, inspirational and have universal appeal. We hope you agree as well.

Justine Boyd
Board member,
YWCA of Greater Atlanta and
past president, Atlanta-Fulton County
League of Women Voters

Ayesha Khanna
CEO, YWCA of Greater Atlanta

Acknowledgements

Atlanta Women Speak would not have been possible without the help of the following individuals:

Becky Blalock, vice president of community and economic development, Georgia Power, and president-elect of the YWCA of Greater Atlanta, for executive support and corporate sponsorship of the book.

Emelyne Mosier, community and economic development, Georgia Power, for overall project coordination and for her dedication to the success of this endeavor.

Jim Barber, corporate communications, Georgia Power, for his invaluable production assistance and service on the editorial board.

Additional editorial board members Mary Styles, Tomika DePriest and Jeremy Wilson, for the many hours spent polishing texts.

Patti Raburn, Georgia Power, for administrative assistance, always above and beyond, and Scott Kasselmann, Jane Hill and Ann Monahan for production assistance.

David M. Ratcliffe, president and CEO, and Art McClung, manager of corporate relations, Georgia Power; Ingrid Saunders Jones, senior vice president, and Helen Price, assistant vice president, The Coca-Cola Company; Harriette Watkins, vice president, AGL Resources; Michael Ross, president and CEO, MHR International; Dr. C. Clayton Powell, Development Authority of Fulton County; Dorothy Harris, president, D. Clark Harris; Karen Elaine Webster, senior corporate vice president, BEERS Skanska; and Nathaniel Ford, general manager, and Alice T. Wiggins, assistant general manager of external affairs, MARTA, for corporate sponsorship of the book; Mary Ann Gaunt and Audrey Hines for their individual sponsorship.

Jeff Lanier and Eric Frank, Heidelberg USA Inc., and Meade Paper for printing the book pro bono.

Linda Jordan, president of the YWCA of Greater Atlanta, for individual sponsorship.

Mara Holley, co-president of the Atlanta-Fulton County League of Women Voters and YWCA of Greater Atlanta Development chair, for individual sponsorship.

Brenda Foye Cornelius, co-president of the Atlanta-Fulton County League of Women Voters.

Their leadership is the light that guides our ship.

Justine & Ayesha

ACKNOWLEDGEMENTS

AWS Committee Members:
Brigitte Bailey
Douglass Bell
Becky Blalock
Justine Boyd, chair
LOLITA BROWNING
Faith Carmichael
Brenda Foye Cornelius
Maureen Darcey
Katherine Diamandis
Nonie Ebeling
Deborah Schwartz-Griffin
Dorothy Harris
Mara Holley
Sheila Hudson
Linda Jordan
Mike Kayembe
Ayesha Khanna
Kathy Klatt, co-chair
Diane Powell-Larché
Mary Long
Cheryl McClellan
Vickie Newton
Laurie Grant Nichols
Cecilia Houston-Torrance
Sherri Wright

Proceeds from this book will help fund the missions of the Atlanta-Fulton County League of Women Voters and the YWCA of Greater Atlanta. To order additional copies, please call 404-577-8683 or send your mailing address and a $30 check or money order, (per book, includes shipping and handling) payable to Atlanta Women Speak, to:
    Atlanta Women Speak
    c/o League of Women Voters
    75 Piedmont Ave., Suite 348
    Atlanta, GA 30303

ATLANTA Women Speak

SPEECHES ON IMPORTANT ISSUES
BY PROMINENT ATLANTA WOMEN

Edited by Em Mosier

with assistance from Jim Barber

Foreword by The Honorable Shirley Franklin, Mayor of Atlanta

Joanna Adams

Joanna Adams is senior pastor of Trinity Presbyterian Church in northwest Atlanta. With a membership of over 2,000, Trinity is the largest church in the Presbyterian Church, USA, with a woman as senior pastor.

Adams serves on the board of directors of The Rockdale Foundation Inc., the board of visitors of Emory University and the board of trustees of the Trinity School. She is a member of the Women's Forum of Atlanta and is a graduate of Leadership DeKalb and Leadership Atlanta. She is also the founding chairperson of the Atlanta Area Task Force on Homelessness, as well as the founding president and vice president of Our House Day Shelter for Homeless Children.

A native of Atlanta, Adams is married to attorney Alfred B. Adams III. They have two grown children, Elizabeth and Sam, and one granddaughter, Virginia.

BUILDING BRIDGES IN THE 21ST CENTURY: BETWEEN RICH AND POOR

*Joanna Adams to the congregation of
Trinity Presbyterian Church (Excerpts)*
Atlanta — January, 2000

A recent *New Yorker* cartoon has two men walking down a city street. They have just passed a homeless man standing with his hat held out to them for a donation. One guy says to the other guy, "Here I was all this time worrying that I was a selfish person. Now it turns out that I'm only suffering from compassion fatigue." (January 10, 2000) Now a cartoon is just a cartoon, but one has to wonder if this one has not tapped into one of the most alarming trends of our times, which I would describe as a deepening indifference to the poor.

Hardly anyone talks about the poor and the left-out anymore. The assumption, I guess, is that in our booming economy, there are no more poor people, but that is simply not the case. Twenty percent of our fellow citizens — including 15 million children — live at or below the poverty line. Lack of access to healthcare bars more than 40 million Americans from reliable and timely healthcare treatment. The underclass in America continues to grow, even as the number of millionaires and billionaires skyrockets. There are now 170 billionaires in the United States, as opposed to 13 in 1982. This growing chasm between rich and poor is not unique to the United States. It is a worldwide trend. The world's income distribution is like the shape of a champagne glass, in which the richest fifth receives 82.7 percent of the world's income, while the poorest fifth receives 1.4 percent.

Why aren't we talking about this? One reason is that it is so easy to become cocooned in our own worlds, our own lives and lifestyles, that we assume that everyone else is living as we do. Another reason is that individualism is so ingrained into our psyches that we are losing our grip on the concepts of community and social justice. Rather than building bridges, we are busy building walls and putting up gates and upgrading our security systems. But surely we all realize that a society that works for only a few will not work for any for long.

In the Old Testament, concern for the poor and left-out is the second most prominent theme, after idolatry. Time and again, the prophets warn the people, "Your cities are not going to survive if you neglect the widow and the orphan." In the New Testament, the subject of poverty and the responsibility of wealth are found in one out of every 10 verses in the first three gospels and in one out of every seven in the Gospel of Luke.

> *It is not the role of religion to solve complex economic and social problems. Religion's contribution is to make sure that the right questions are being asked.*

Why does the Bible give so much attention to these matters? An obvious answer is that those to whom the writings were first addressed must have had a difficult time wrapping their heads around the idea of how one treated one's neighbor was of eternal importance. Fairness and compassion are not ancillary aspects of the Christian gospel; they were and always will be the heart of the gospel. We need to care about the well-being of more than just ourselves and our own families.

Let me reflect for a moment on the current state of affairs in modern society. It has been suggested that we are currently undergoing the third dramatic societal change in human history. The first great transformation occurred when small, nomadic tribes settled down in impermanent villages and then in towns and cities, and life became based on agriculture and domestication of animals. Thousands of years passed until the second transformation, which took place only 200 years ago with the Industrial Revolution. Now the suggestion is that we are in the midst of the third great societal transformation in human history, as we move into an information-, knowledge-based, post-industrial society ruled by free-market capitalism. The changes being wrought are altering forever the relationship of people to their work. The changes are leaving in their wake both winners and losers.

It is not the role of religion to solve complex economic and social problems. Religion's contribution is to make sure that the right questions are being asked: Who is being left out and what can be done about it? What sort of global society do we want, since a global society is the society we are going to have? What, if any, are the moral boundaries of accumulating wealth? What is being done to ensure the dignity of all human persons?

Individualism and free capitalism are two of the hallmarks of the American way, but they are not the only hallmarks. There are other qualities of our heritage grown in the rich soil of our religious traditions that we must not lose sight of.

Justice and mercy are deeply imbedded in the American way. The American (Martin Luther King Jr.) our nation honors tomorrow also realized the dangers of rampant individualism and the necessity of having the capacity to feel compassion for an other human being.

This also is the American way — to love our neighbors as much as we love ourselves. It was also Christ's way. One day he told a story about a rich man who was dressed in purple — this was an expensive cloth dyed with liquid obtained from a rare shellfish. Only the most elite could afford to clothe themselves in purple. Every day he feasted sumptuously. At the gate of his house, there lay a poor man named Lazarus who longed to satisfy his hunger with what fell from the rich man's table. The poor man died. The rich man died, too. The rich man left it all and went to Hades; the poor man was carried away by angels to be with Abraham. The rich man cried to Abraham, "Please send Lazarus to dip the tip of his finger in water to cool my tongue," but Abraham said, "In life, you had everything, but now the tables have been turned."

Notice that the rich man is not condemned for being rich. He is not judged for being very rich. The only thing that he is judged for is not seeing his neighbor. In fact, the first time he ever acknowledges Lazarus' existence is when he asks for help with his thirst. The rich man's problem was that he allowed his prosperity to blind him, to limit his vision. He pulled down the shades, retreated into his private world and never noticed his neighbor.

In yesterday's *Constitution*, there was a column written by my long-time friend, Mark Bashor. Mark is a scientist at the national Centers for Disease Control, and he has worked as a volunteer with homeless people for 20 years. His beautiful column ended with this rhetorical question: "Even if we cannot invite everyone inside our privileged society, is it not time, at least, to invite everyone simply inside?"

Inspired by his column, I dug around in my files and I found a letter that Mark had written to me in April 1986. At the time, I was following the progress of a homeless man named Randy, who had won and lost many battles with alcoholism. Mark and his wife, Katie, had taken a personal interest in Randy, so much so that they decided that if Randy was ever going to get anywhere, he would have to get out of the shelter and come to stay at their house in Decatur for a while. Mark's letter was written to me two months after Randy had gone to live with Mark and Katie and their then 1-year-old toddler named Ryan.

> Dear Joanna,
>
> It occurred to me after you called last night that there is another part of the Ryan-and-Randy saga that Katie and I enjoy watching ... [Randy the alcoholic-African-American-homeless man and Ryan their 1-year-old son], and I don't think we've shared that with you yet.
>
> Two or three nights a week, Randy's work schedule, together with his dependence on MARTA for transportation to and from his job, and Ryan's bath and bed schedule, result in Randy's getting home just about the time the three of us are finishing our dinner.
>
> Ryan almost immediately wants out of his high chair, whether he's finished eating or not, and he goes and sits in Randy's lap while Randy eats (while Kate and I clean off the table, start straightening the kitchen, etc.).
>
> While the two of them sit there at the table, Ryan continues eating, but from Randy's plate. And every now and then, Ryan gets a slimy fistful of food and holds it up to Randy's mouth, insisting with a little "grunt" that Randy eat whatever it is that he's offering. Randy obligingly eats whatever is offered, even though it's covered with baby-drool!
>
> Every time I watch this, I am reminded of the story of the man who prayed that God would show him the meaning of the Lord's Supper. I have seen it at my own kitchen table.
>
> Love, Mark

There is a great chasm in this world between the rich and poor, but with God's help and with the grace of Christ, it can be crossed. Thanks be to God.

Judy Anderson

Judy Anderson is senior vice president of Georgia Power, serving as president of the Georgia Power Foundation and the Southern Company Charitable Foundation. Both foundations are ranked among Georgia's top charitable organizations in giving.

Anderson is on the board of directors of Camp Best Friends, the Alliance Theatre Company and Fernbank Inc. She is a member of the Rotary Club of Atlanta, the American Bar Association, the Georgia State Bar Association and the International Women's Forum, Georgia chapter. In 1997, she was named the YWCA's Woman of Achievement.

Anderson also has served on the boards of the Atlanta Urban League, Junior Achievement of Georgia and the Piedmont Park Conservancy. Her fund-raising efforts have benefited many organizations, including the Woodruff Arts Center, the United Way of Metropolitan Atlanta and the American Red Cross.

THE BUSINESS OF GIVING
Judy Anderson to The Southern Council of Foundations
Atlanta — February, 2002

Philanthropy is big business for big business. The latest records available, for the year 1999, show that corporate foundations contributed almost $3 billion to America's non-profit organizations. And that figure represents more than a 20 percent increase from the previous year.

Indeed, growth in corporate contributions in the United States has been on a steady upward course for many years, despite economic ups and downs and other factors that have affected corporate earnings. Still another plus, corporations worldwide are beginning to follow America's lead and devoting increasing emphasis and financial support to community-based organizations.

At the risk of sounding somewhat self-serving, perhaps they are recognizing what Georgia Power has known – and practiced – since its earliest days: that supporting the community you serve is not only the right thing to do, but the business "centsable" thing to do.

Preston Arkwright, one of Georgia Power's earliest presidents, articulated this company philosophy in 1926 when he delivered a speech entitled, "A Citizen Wherever We Serve." The phrase quickly was adopted throughout the company and still stands today, not only as a corporate motto, but also as a guidepost for conducting our business day in and day out.

What Georgia Power and other corporations also have learned about lending their support to non-profit organizations is that these efforts are positively received by customers, whose views are, of course, always of critical importance. Of great significance, too, is the fact that employees tend to feel a stronger connection and greater loyalty to their company and their community when a strong, clearly visible corporate contribution program is in place. And that's good for everyone concerned.

The focus of corporate givers, through their foundations, has been undergoing some significant changes in recent years. Non-profits need to understand these changes and take every opportunity to use them to their greatest advantage.

First and foremost, corporations now are seeking non-profit organizations that are ready and willing to work in partnership with them. That means non-profits must recognize that corporations want to do more than simply provide money. While financial contributions are still at the heart of corporate support, companies can and want to make a growing range of resources available, including facilities for meetings; loaned employees who can work on boards, special projects and task forces for a designated period; and company volunteers who can get involved on their own time and help sustain various programs.

Second, corporations are focusing more and more on directing their support toward organizations whose goals and programs are in alignment with one or more of the corporation's own goals and concerns, as well as the needs of the community at large. For example, one of the primary issues for Georgia Power today is the recruitment of our future work force. We care greatly about the development of a large pool of young people in Georgia that is diverse in its make-up, educated and eager to pursue productive careers.

This is a corporate goal that benefits the entire community, so it makes sense from every standpoint to target entities that provide education and education-related programs as major recipients of our corporate giving and support.

Many of our corporate goals – and much of the work we do – also are concentrated on environmental issues. Here again is an area that is important to our company and to the community we serve. Accordingly, we are looking to bolster the efforts and provide resources for those non-profit organizations that are involved in work related to improving the air and water quality in our state, preserving our natural resources and protecting endangered species.

The emphasis on education and environment represents a substantive change in direction for our corporate giving, since much of our past support has gone to health and human services. However, we are maintaining a very strong commitment to the United Way and rely on that organization to address the needs in health and human services. Their agencies are solidly linked to communities at the grassroots level.

The lesson in this example of Georgia Power's current priorities for corporate giving is that non-profits need to gain a clear understanding of the strategic direction and goals of potential corporate donors. If there is a fit between corporate concerns and the non-profit's own objectives, then the chances of establishing a meaningful, mutually beneficial relationship are far greater. If there isn't a fit, the non-profit needs to look to other donors, while keeping in mind that priorities change and corporations periodically assess the issues they face and redefine their direction as appropriate.

It's important to note that the move to more strategic giving is likely to result in corporations providing larger amounts of support to a fewer number of organizations than once was the case. With the larger amounts of support will come even closer, more thoughtful examinations of the entities that are recipients.

The reason is simple. When more resources are invested, there are greater expectations from senior management and shareholders concerning the effectiveness of the funding being provided.

How can non-profit organizations help ensure they are meeting these expectations? By establishing well-thought-out mission statements and objectives; by developing both operational and strategic plans that incorporate methods for measuring results and long-term progress; and by presenting meaningful information about their programs and activities – including the good news and the bad!

All of this material helps corporate decision-makers feel confident in the funding choices they make, and helps protect corporate giving programs at a time when businesses are constantly pressured to improve the efficiency and effectiveness of all aspects of their operations.

While we may shift our emphasis on philanthropic support in the non-profit community, our commitment to providing a leadership role in corporate giving remains. Our long experience in community service and giving has made clear the great good that corporations and their employees can do in enhancing the overall quality of life in the cities and towns we serve throughout Georgia.

We want to use that experience and knowledge to bring more businesses into the fold of corporate donors, and to increase the level of support provided by corporations that already have charitable giving programs in place.

That's why Georgia Power and its executives don't hesitate to bring together people from the corporate side and non-profit side to learn about and explore issues and problems. We do this in meetings small and large, formal and informal, because we are confident that if we create opportunities for people from diverse backgrounds to meet and work together, new partnerships will be forged, new programs will be started and existing programs will gain greater understanding and support.

We also don't hesitate to issue challenges. A few years ago, we urged other corporations to become involved in the YWCA, and to demonstrate their commitment as we were doing by providing matching contributions when new members joined the YWCA. Our challenge was taken up by The Coca-Cola Company, resulting in thousands of dollars of additional funding for the YWCA that would not otherwise have been provided.

Corporate giving programs and the full breadth of resources they offer – plus the thousands and thousands of corporate volunteers, plus the staff of hundreds and hundreds of non-profit organizations – represent so many and so much that their combined impact can exceed even the greatest hopes.

And if corporate donors and non-profits alike need expertise in fund-raising, we stand ready to help. Our executives and managers have led many of the most successful fund-raising campaigns ever undertaken for non-profit organizations in Atlanta and throughout Georgia, and we welcome the opportunity to share what we have learned.

It is popular now to talk about the power of one – and rightly so. However, the power of many is also tremendous, especially when channeled toward making our community a better place to live. Corporate giving programs and the full breadth of resources they offer – plus the thousands and thousands of corporate volunteers, plus the staff of hundreds and hundreds of non-profit organizations – represent so many and so much that their combined impact can exceed even the greatest hopes. It's an exciting prospect, and one that, together, we can bring to realization.

Atlanta is a pacesetter for the country in corporate giving, and is fortunate to have major corporate contributors such as The Coca-Cola Company, Georgia Power and many others who reflect being a citizen wherever they serve. As individuals, Atlantans have a long-time willingness to support good works and causes, including our successful efforts to bring the 1996 Centennial Olympic Games to our city.

To be as successful as possible, those who lead corporate giving programs should adopt a bold, ambitious vision and set objectives that bring people together and generate excitement and energy. They should have self-confidence to inspire others, and self-criticism to constantly recognize the need for change and improvement. And they should constantly seek to do more.

In conclusion, I encourage you to make corporate philanthropy a hallmark of your company and community support a part of your own life. You'll find the rewards far exceed the resources you dedicate.

Kathy Ashe

Kathy Ashe represents the 46th District in the Georgia House of Representatives. First elected to the House in 1991, Ashe serves on the Appropriations, Education, MARTOC and Ways and Means Committees. She is an active member of the Women's Caucus, and last year became Georgia's legislative appointee to the Southern Regional Education Board.

Ashe is a graduate of Leadership Atlanta and the Regional Leadership Institute. She serves on the boards of Research Atlanta, the Atlanta Women's Foundation and the Wellesley Centers for Women. She also serves on the Agnes Scott College board of trustees, where she is a member of the Executive Committee.

Ashe is also an Elder of Central Presbyterian Church, where she teaches kindergarten Sunday School. She is married to attorney Lawrence Ashe. They have two grown children, Robbie and Sally.

OF SUITCASES AND CANDLES

Kathy Ashe to the Trinity School 6th Grade Graduation

Atlanta — June, 1999

I invite you to think about two images that I would like for you to take away from this celebration. First, imagine a suitcase. As you leave Trinity School and begin a new journey, you take with you a suitcase of experiences and relationships.

Although each of your suitcases is uniquely your own, you have some very special shared items, experiences with the concept of community and experiences with the stewardship of Peachtree Creek as River Kids. The list goes on.

As you take these suitcases with you, there are four things I would ask you to think about:

1) On this special day remember to salute and thank the folks who have helped you pack your suitcase. Remember to thank the folks of Trinity because each of you has a special teacher or two without whom you might not be here today. Your parents and family members deserve your thanks for their love and faith in you and your abilities. Your religious traditions and beliefs have had an impact on the decisions about what you have packed to take with you. Your friends, the folks you have played ball with, sweated through exams with, and shared secrets with, all are a part of the suitcase you take with you. Remember to be appreciative.

2) Be willing to acknowledge that your suitcase has room for the experiences and relationships that you will add to it. Save room to encounter the new and the challenging. Save room to take advantage of the opportunities that await you at the next school, the next chance to learn something new. You wouldn't leave on a vacation without room for souvenirs you hope to accumulate. Be willing to brave the future and enjoy it.

3) Be willing to dig around in your suitcase to find what you need. On days when you wonder how to get through what faces you, remember the experiences and relationships you have stowed away and seek help. Your Trinity friends will be there for you and available even when your paths are far apart. Just like you have had to dig around to find clean socks or underwear, know that you have family, faith and school experiences and relationships for days that look bright or bleak.

4) Be willing to interact with the "stuff" that you accumulate in your suitcase and be willing to discard that which no longer serves you well – be it a habit that holds you back or a friend who leads you in the wrong direction. Be willing to take responsibility for your decisions and live with the consequences, even when it is tough. Don't hang on to junk!

Just like your fingerprints, what is in your suitcase is unique. Value yourself and let your light shine.

The second image is the image of your light — your candle. You know the song, "This little light of mine, I'm gonna let it shine." (On another day, I'll tell you about the history of that simple and yet complex little song and its relationship to the Civil Rights movement). Your light, the light that is uniquely you, can't be hidden under a bushel. It has the power to improve the quality of whatever communities in which you find yourself: your family, camp this summer, your next school.

> *Just like your fingerprints,*
> *what is in your suitcase is unique.*
> *Value yourself and let your light shine.*

Each of you is special on this day of celebration and transition. I salute you: the uniqueness of the suitcase you have packed and the uniqueness of your light. As you leave this wonderful school, know that the experiences gained, the skills mastered, the friendships earned, go with you.

Know that your light shines and that, on dark days, it has the ability to light your path. It helps you find guidance in making tough decisions, and lends you the strength to do what needs to be done. And on bright, joyous days (like this one), your light adds its own special shine to the brilliance all around. Your light is not diminished by other lights, but adds its own sparkle.

Be willing to take responsibility for your decisions and live with the consequences, even when it is tough. Don't hang on to junk!

Let me end by saying congratulations to each of you! Individually and collectively, you set this world ablaze!

Jacquelyn H. Barrett

Jacquelyn H. Barrett is currently serving her third consecutive term as sheriff of Fulton County. She was the first African-American female in the country elected to the office of sheriff.

Barrett is a recipient of the Martin Luther King Jr. Drum Major for Justice Award and the Jean Young Community Service Award. In 1995, she was inducted into the Atlanta YWCA's Academy of Women. She is a graduate of Leadership Atlanta and continues to work with the organization's Alumni Association. She is also past president of the National Organization of Black Law Enforcement Executives, and was appointed by Governor Roy Barnes to the Board of Public Safety for the State of Georgia.

Barrett is the mother of two grown children.

JACQUELYN H. BARRETT

MAKING A DIFFERENCE NO MATTER WHERE WE SERVE
Jackie Barrett to The Possible Woman® Leadership Conference
(Excerpts)
Negril, Jamaica — January, 2001

As I begin my third term as sheriff of Fulton County, I can share some stories with you about many fascinating things, and some not so fascinating. Many of the stories that I may tell you are sprinkled with facts about such problems that seem to plague all of our communities – gang violence, teenage prostitution, drugs, homicide, poverty and homelessness. We all face these problems no matter where we are — or no matter where we serve people. After all, that's what leadership is all about, serving others.

It was Dr. Martin Luther King Jr. who said, "Everybody can be great, because everybody can serve." I believe he was talking about every one here because in some big or small way, we have been chosen to serve others. Whether we have arrived in our roles by elections, appointments, promotions, mergers or entrepreneurial dreams, we have been chosen to carry the torch of leadership.

And so, tonight, I want to talk to you about "Making A Difference No Matter Where You Serve."

Service is a noble duty and high calling. It is a privilege to serve others. Sometimes, our roles as leaders and lawmakers conflict with the convictions of our hearts. It is then that we face the "test" of doing the right thing regardless of popular votes or popular opinion.

Each of us at one time faces an opportunity that makes us create a balance between career and life experiences. However great the challenges, I believe we can make a difference no matter where we serve.

Your everyday experiences may take you to the streets of Atlanta, Chicago, New York or wherever you live or serve. Frankly, it doesn't matter where we serve; there are similar stories in all of our professions.

You may not have to confront a young gang member, but there is a young person, male or female, who dares you and me to step away from the badge or boardroom to listen and advise. Sometimes, we can help the situation; sometimes, we can't. What's important is that we attempt to make a difference no matter where we serve.

There is a biblical text that we have all heard at some point in our career. It says: "To whom much is given, much is required." That is the mantra that should guide the servant leaders in this room. We have been given much, but it is to be shared … with hundreds and thousands of people.

We are leaders for our country – America – or wherever we live. I believe that as servant leaders, we are not limited by geographic boundaries, skin color, ethnicity or gender.

So what is my message? I challenge us to examine our real priorities and see where we have room for a young person who may be struggling to grow in the right direction. Yes, I understand that our plates are full and our cups run over.

But as America prepares for a new administration under President-elect George W. Bush, I want to encourage you to listen closely to what's happening in Washington. We cannot afford to be silent or sleep and allow individuals to be confirmed for the Cabinet who are not sensitive to all people everywhere. Our country must deal with racial profiling, gun control, a woman's right to choose (pro-choice), poverty, education and healthcare.

If we are to survive the 21st Century, then we have to demand leadership from Washington and local government that places people before politics and personal gain. These critical issues must remain on the radar if we are to remain a strong nation, a strong community and a strong people.

What convictions do you have that are unshakable? How far will you go to help a person in need – given your profile as a leader in your community? How can you give a voice to another woman or even a man who desperately needs you to make a difference wherever you serve?

These are not easy questions for any of us; yet, leaders are confronted with tough questions during tough times. These are not easy times to serve. Everybody seems to have some file or another on your life. Many great skillful leaders shy away from public office because the scrutiny is too much for their families.

I would like to close by reminding us that we are the voices for those who are not able to speak in Washington or wherever the decisions are made. We are the ones who must make their voices heard about better healthcare. There are too many elderly mothers and fathers who worry about their future because they cannot afford the medicine and healthcare that they so desperately need. They need our voices.

There are too many children who cannot read, and they are slipping through the cracks in our schools. The road they're on will lead them from the classroom to the streets because they will not be prepared for college or the work force. They need our voices.

There are too many black men and other ethnic groups who are victims of racial profiling because the ugly mold of racism has not been broken. There are too many women who are denied opportunities of leadership because the ugly mold of sexism has not been removed.

In America, we have the freedom of expression. You can say just about anything – within reason of course. But the point I want to make is that, as women in particular, we can speak. Our voices are not silenced.

I wish the story were the same for women everywhere. There are women in other parts of the world whose voices are silenced by laws and traditions.

They would give their lives – in some instances – to experience The POSSIBLE WOMAN Conference. But that's not a reality for many of them.

Let us leave this Conference with a renewed spirit to go back to our cities and countries to speak up for those who are silenced.

Let us reach out for troubled children or people within our reach – who may need our leadership beyond the titles we wear.

Let us remember that we have been chosen to lead in these difficult times. It is not only a gift; it is a high calling. The phenomenal truth is that each of us has the tools, resources and power to lead.

Most of all, let us remember to prepare others around us for new leadership. Therefore, we must not only lead, but we are charged to make leaders of the men and women who serve under our leadership.

We are the women and men who have been chosen to make a difference wherever we serve!

Linda Bell

Linda Bell is a professor of philosophy and the director of the Women's Studies Institute at Georgia State University. In addition to feminist theory, she teaches and writes in the areas of existentialism, ethics and continental philosophy.

Bell has published several books in these areas of expertise, including *Visions of Women*, an anthology of philosophers' statements about women; *Sartre's Ethics of Authenticity*, a development of an ethics from the writings of Jean-Paul Sartre; and *Rethinking Ethics in the Midst of Violence: A Feminist Approach to Freedom*, an existentialist approach to feminist ethics. She is currently developing a collection of essays dealing with aspects of her own experience and how they play a role in her philosophizing.

AN AFFIRMATIVE-ACTION POSTER PROFESSOR
*Linda Bell to the Southern Humanities Council
Conference on Justice (Excerpts)*
Montgomery, Alabama — March, 1998

It was 1970, and most colleges and universities around the country weren't particularly concerned about hiring women, except perhaps to avoid doing so. Still, I was being interviewed for a temporary teaching position at Georgia State University.

Though my previous two years of part-time teaching had been relatively uneventful, I should have known that additional years might be more turbulent when its president, interviewing me for a full-time position, began to yell, "If you think Georgia State is on its way and hasn't arrived, then you obviously don't belong here!"

I guess I responded adequately to the ensuing harangue. I didn't cry, run, get angry or scream back at him. In fact, I probably didn't even respond in any way that might have suggested that his attempt at intimidation had been effective. In any event, I was hired.

At the end of the second year, I packed up all the books and files in my office and left, resolved to finish my dissertation while living on the refund of my retirement contributions. Then and only then would I again worry about how I would support myself, given that the academic market for philosophers had become glutted while I had been in graduate school.

With my dissertation almost done at the end of the summer, I was surprised to receive a call from the chairman. On learning that I had not found a job for the coming year, he inquired if I would like to teach again at Georgia State. In response to my questions, he explained that the dean was feeling some pressure to increase the extremely low number of women faculty in the college and, learning that I had just been let go, had expressed his concern. Seizing the unanticipated opportunity to increase the size of the department, the chairman had quickly contacted me.

Of course, I accepted, even though I knew it would delay the completion of my dissertation by a few more months. I had, after all, been envisioning waiting tables. For a klutz like me, that had seemed a daunting prospect.

When I hear people today bemoaning the psychological harm affirmative action does to its alleged beneficiaries, I find myself thinking of this less than auspicious beginning of my teaching career at Georgia State. While my ego wasn't in the best shape it's ever been in, only beginning to recover from my father's suicide, my divorce and my earlier graduate school disaster at Northwestern, I had been able to compare myself with other graduate students in philosophy and had seen enough of the profession to realize that I was at least as bright and as philosophically adept as many others who were coming along or who had made it in academe. From the time I first applied to graduate schools in philosophy and had been rejected by most, while male classmates with lower grades than my almost straight-A average had been accepted with handsome fellowship offers, my gender had been only a disadvantage, overshadowing any consideration of merit. Instead of questioning my ability, I thought of my previous struggles and decided that the affirmative action that created my tenure-track position was an appropriate and long-delayed tribute to the fact that I had persevered in spite of the sexism I had encountered.

As one of the beneficiaries of affirmative action, I can truthfully say that my academic life has been difficult — but not because of affirmative action. Opponents, with their self-fulfilling prophecies disingenuously disguised as concern, are quite right that individuals hired because of pressures on an institution with a long history of racism and sexism are likely to be seen as inferior, no matter how accomplished they may be. The disingenuous aspect of this concern becomes evident, though, when one realizes that without the affirmative action those who might have benefited from such hiring would have continued to be seen as inferior, but without the jobs and the consequent opportunities to prove themselves.

So I have tried to ignore those who question whether I would have gotten my job apart from affirmative action. I know very well that the answer is no. Moreover, I am quite confident that this doesn't reflect on my ability, one way or the other, convinced as I am that it simply didn't matter how good I was as a philosopher. I've seen far too many brilliant women passed over in job searches where relatively mediocre men were selected to think for a minute that merit rules in academic hiring.

As it turned out, affirmative action did little for me beyond opening the door to a position. When I was evaluated for tenure and promotion, it became apparent not only that the chairman had seen my hiring as a way to increase the number of faculty positions in the department but also that he had no intention of keeping me, regardless of how I performed.

> *I have tried to ignore those who question whether I would have gotten my job apart from affirmative action. I know very well that the answer is no. Moreover, I am quite confident that this doesn't reflect on my ability*

Thus, five years later, as my tenure evaluation began, he affirmed that he wanted my position and one other to be "revolving doors" so that the department could avoid the alleged hazard of being "over-tenured," one of the chairman's big concerns as he continually talked, albeit in mixed metaphors, about the need for "fresh blood." The mention of fresh blood led me to imagine my colleagues as vampires by night and perhaps by day as well, satisfied only by draining the life out of young philosophers.

Although I had managed to publish several articles while teaching the standard but extraordinarily heavy load of classes, the department evaluated my publications as adequate in quantity but not in quality and concluded that I did not merit tenure and promotion at Georgia State. Only one of the tenured members of the department wrote a minority report supporting me. Another, who had signed the majority decision, told me later that he had been "on my side" and wanted me to understand that he "had to sign." Of course, I didn't understand.

Facing so united a front, I had little hope of winning an appeal, especially since I had made myself rather unpopular with the administration by opposing, openly and sometimes with success, an embarrassingly constructed and very backward set of statutes the administration was pushing for the university. On the other hand, I had little hope of finding another position in philosophy, given the tight job market and given that I would be applying after having been denied tenure by an institution as lacking in prestige as was Georgia State at that time. Besides, I really didn't want to find another position since I had enjoyed teaching the students at this university. They were often such fun to have in philosophy courses, bright, iconoclastic, generally older than the traditional college age, and interested in the questions.

At any rate, feeling I had little to lose and using an appeal process that had just been established, I challenged the department's and chairman's recommendations against tenure and promotion, using their emphasis on the issue of quality as I wrote to individuals who had published what I regarded as the best work in the areas of my papers. Though such outside reviews are now routinely sought in promotion and tenure cases throughout the country, they were not then, so far as I know, and certainly not at Georgia State. Trying not to pressure in any way the philosophers whose evaluations I sought, I simply explained that in my promotion and tenure evaluation the quality of my publications was in dispute. I asked each of them to read the article(s) in his or her area of expertise and to comment on its (or their) worth. All but one generously agreed to do so and wrote positive evaluations.

During the time of the appeal, I knew my behavior had to be impeccably professional, that a lot of people were watching and waiting for a slip in comportment that they could point to as compelling grounds for sending me on my way. However much I worried about keeping my job, I dared not mention my predicament or manifest my anxieties in any way when talking with students. I had seen others castigated for "unprofessional" conduct — namely, "recruiting" support — because students had challenged dismissals of their instructors. I felt I couldn't risk even one speaking up for me. However demoralized I was as the result of being judged so harshly, I dared not let it show so that psychological instability or some such accusation could be used against me. However angry I was at those self-righteous colleagues and at that chair, at least several of whom could not themselves have met the standards they were invoking against me, I knew I would lose were I to tell some of them exactly what I thought of the quality of their published work and how outraged I was that trees had lost their lives to make it possible.

Even my letter of appeal had to be worded carefully so that it contained none of the ad hominems that were so tempting and that felt so soul-satisfying to write. I simply could not state or write anything impugning motivations no matter how much I thought they needed to be impugned. A friend helped me excise these from my appeal, meeting my heart-felt resistance to each excision with the wise words, "Linda, do you want to win or get even?" As much as I wanted to do both, I knew as well as he that my behavior and not theirs was at issue and that I had to proceed with extreme caution. No wonder that by the end of the process I had moved into a depression for which I needed and sought medical help; but, of course, this was just something else I had to keep hidden.

I won the appeal. Once the depression was successfully treated, all I had to do was be a gracious winner. While even that was sometimes difficult, knowing the support I had received from friends, as well as from philosophers whose work I admired, made the aftermath of this stressful time much easier.

While earlier it had been intensely difficult to hold my head high and feel part of a department that didn't want me and didn't value my work, I continued to control my reactions but with far less effort, even managing not to gloat when the chairman suddenly decided to retire, professing that his job just wasn't "as much fun" as it used to be. I resisted the sarcasm of observing that losing power must never be easy — or fun.

Yes, I fought to get into and to stay in academe. Moreover, it took me a couple of decades and the rank of professor before I began occasionally, but still somewhat hesitantly, to use "we" when I spoke either of the department and the university in particular or of philosophy and academe in general. Sometimes, I still feel like I'm odd-person-out, and not without reason, since I remain painfully aware that several in the department haven't budged from the opinion of me that they voiced back then. They've never come to presentations I've given, and I suspect they've never read carefully — or perhaps at all — anything I've written, probably not even those early articles they judged lacking in quality so many years ago. I know that my support for a candidate or for a proposal all too frequently gives them sufficient reason to vote on the other side. Because of that, I try not to say anything when my suggestions receive serious attention — only after being made as though for the first time by a male colleague. If I don't keep quiet, I jeopardize that attention. While I wish this scenario weren't such a frequent one, I know from talking with women in other departments that I'm not the only one to whom it happens and that it's not just because of the way I was hired or the dispute over my promotion and tenure.

Nevertheless, I've survived and even thrived in academe. I've had a chance to do some things that were very important to me, including developing and publishing my ideas for others to read. And like most, I didn't do it alone. I've been encouraged and even mentored by some fair-minded men in philosophy — almost all, however, outside my department. I've experienced the generosity and care of friends, both female and male, without which I probably wouldn't have survived. Those connected with Women's Studies at Georgia State — from its less than auspicious beginning through its battles against entrenched and powerful opposition to its recent recognition as an Institute — have been and continue to be the heart of my academic life-support system. There, I find a group of academics who exemplify the willingness to question, the excitement about ideas and the life of the mind, and the intellectual give and take that initially lured me into philosophy and academe.

Best of all, having become director of the Women's Studies Institute at Georgia State and playing a somewhat more central role than earlier in its continuing development, I find myself delighted that I was able to endure through the earlier struggles and to live long enough to see things change to some extent. Now I can actually experience occasional academic situations in which women are important and sometimes key players and in which race and gender, even class, are taken seriously. Now I can and do very proudly say "we," about the Institute, about its collaboration with the library as we acquire papers from women's movements, do oral interviews with the women who were part of them, and work for funding for lecture series and research, and about the wonderful donors, of collections and of money, as we work together to advance the position of women in the archives, in the university and in the world.

Now I can see positive consequences of my often disheartening struggles and no longer am limited to battles the success of which is likely to be just the prevention of a worst-case scenario. There are, of course, still many such battles, and they remain discouraging. Only those who have endured similar struggles can really understand just how good it feels that those are no longer the only ones.

Juel Pate Borders-Benson

Rev. Dr. Juel Pate Borders-Benson has practiced medicine in Atlanta since 1965. She served as an OB-GYN until 1985, and currently runs a gynecology practice. She is also an associate minister at Wheat Street Baptist Church.

Borders-Benson is a member of the American College of Obstetricians and Gynecologists and the Medical Association of Georgia. She is the co-chairperson of the Heritage Fund of the Atlanta Medical Association and is on the advisory board of the Ultrasound Diagnostics School. She also serves as the sponsor of the Julia Pate Borders Memorial Nurses Guild and is advisor to the non-hearing members and interpreters at Wheat Street Baptist Church.

Borders-Benson has two grown children, Theodore, Jr. and Elinor Maria, with the late Dr. Theodore Benson, Sr., D.D.S. She also has three grandchildren, Heather Marie Benson, the late Theodore Charles Benson, and William Buchanan Benson.

JUEL PATE BORDERS-BENSON

THE UNQUENCHABLE FIRE
*Juel Pate Borders-Benson to the Candler School of Theology,
Emory University (Excepts)*
Atlanta — December, 1989

> *"I baptize you with water for repentance, but he who is coming after me is mightier than I, whose sandals I am not worthy to carry; He will baptize you with the Holy Spirit and with fire. His winnowing fork is in his hand, and he will clear his threshing floor and gather his wheat into the granary, but the chaff he will burn with unquenchable fire."*
> — Matthew 3:11-12

When I read and re-read this passage from Matthew, I struggled with the selection for emphasis. I could preach on John the Baptist, the forerunner, who was the fulfillment of the prophecy in the third verse of the 40th chapter of Isaiah. I could continue to describe him as a person, his preaching in the wilderness, his likeness to the prophet Elijah, or his great following of people from Jerusalem, Judea and the area surrounding the Jordan. As important as these were, they were not the most important parts of this passage.

I read once again the 11th and the 12th verses of the third chapter of Matthew. My eyes fell on the words "unquenchable fire."

FIRE! That's it!

My mind began to race. The Day of the Lord! The Coming of the Lord! The Judgement of the Lord! I quickly flashed back.

It was Friday evening, April 10, 1987, two days before my ordination. Several months before, I had had many telephone conversations with Rev. Dr. Ralph David Abernathy. He was known to be liberal. He was sympathetic to women who were aspiring to become ordained ministers of the gospel of Jesus Christ. He had been unusually kind, but firm. He asked me to prepare for questions in four areas: Conversion, Call, Church Polity and Christian Doctrine. He requested that I secure a copy of Principles and Practices for Baptist Churches by Edward T. Hiscox and know the contents thoroughly. In addition, he gave me an unexpected oral quiz, approximately three weeks before the big day. He intended for his candidate to be prepared.

Now this was the big day, and there was no turning back. Dr. Abernathy was the presiding officer of the Ordination Council. He sat directly in front of me. To my immediate left was the appointed catechizer, Dr. Grady Butler. My 82-year-old father, third generation minister, sat quietly in the southwest corner of the room. Though he had mixed emotions about the step I was now taking, as always, he was there to give me his full support. Of the six other ministers present, two were women – Rev. Dr. Carrie L. George and Rev. Dr. Miley Mae Hemphill.

After much labored discussion, we finally were ready for the questions on Christian doctrine. Dr. George said, "What is your concept of Hell?" I did not consider this a tricky question, but she had been one of the most meticulous examiners, and thus I paused to construct carefully this important answer. Dr. Abernathy, thinking I was unable to respond, came to my rescue by saying, "Just tell us what you have heard your father preach all these years." With great exuberance, I said, "He preaches hell is eternal torment, that state in which you BURN! BURN! BURN!"

We then began to talk about heaven, hell, sin, God's judgement and God's grace.

When I read "unquenchable fire," not only did this cherished memory come into my mind, but also scriptures in Malachi and Second Peter. The great day of reckoning will come. The wheat and the chaff will be separated. The wheat will be saved. The chaff will be burned in the "unquenchable fire!" In the Second Letter of Peter, the disciple of Peter writes of the same fire: "But by the same word, the heavens and earth that now exist have been stored up for fire, being kept until the day of judgement and destruction of ungodly men." (II Peter 3:7)

Is it possible today that we have had enough of just a taste of this unquenchable fire, this torment, this living daily hell? We have dropped below the bottom. Our streets are unsafe. The drug pushers have lured our children from the classroom. Our elders and our babies are abused. Our family structure is destroyed. A battered woman is further victimized by the male-dominated law enforcement and judicial systems. Prejudice and racial, religious and sexual discrimination are everywhere.

Burn? No, Repent!

I want to hope that the world is beginning to hear the right and understand. No, Marcos, you cannot steal from the people and be buried in peace in your homeland. No, to those who would deny freedom of worship in their own churches. No, economic oppression and police brutality are totally unacceptable. No, to those who oppress in China, Africa and elsewhere. The people must be free and equal!

Burn? No, Repent!

I want to believe that we in the United States are beginning to stress more complete accountability. No, medical doctor, you must conform to guidelines and standards of care, or be judged by a disciplinary board. No, women of America, it is better to prevent a pregnancy than to destroy a human life. No, preacher of the gospel, you are not the king of the people, but the shepherd and servant of all.

Burn? No, Repent!

I want to believe that in our personal lives, we are struggling to be "new born again," that we are walking on higher ground, with a new mind and a new heart. I want to believe that we are praying for the strength to forgive others as we ourselves have been forgiven. I want to believe that we are at least trying to do unto others, as we would have them to do unto us. I want to believe that we know to beg for mercy against that great and terrible day of the coming of the Lord.

Burn in the "Unquenchable fire?" Oh, No!

Repent! Repent! Repent!

Nancy A. Boxill

Dr. Nancy A. Boxill has served on the Fulton County Board of Commissioners since her appointment as interim commissioner in 1987. She was elected in subsequent elections beginning in 1998, becoming the first female commissioner and vice chair of the board.

As a commissioner, Boxill has worked to establish the Fulton County Human Services Department. She also initiated a pilot program for second and third-shift childcare and helped ensure disabled access to the Fulton County Administration Building and Judicial Center.

Boxill serves as chair to the National Black Arts Festival board of directors and the Fulton/Atlanta Land Bank Authority, and is a member of the Herndon Foundation board of trustees and the Atlanta Opera board of directors.

THE CRISIS IN HOMELESSNESS
Nancy Boxill to the U.S. Congress Select Committee
Washington, D.C. — February, 1987

Understanding the effects of homelessness on children begins with understanding the context of their lives. What I want to do is summarize for you the daily life of children who live in shelters in Atlanta.

The day begins when the children are awakened by their mothers at 5:00 a.m. In a cavernous and yet crowded gym, the children help their mothers dissemble their bedding, store their bedding, get dressed, pack their belongings and hope to receive a cold snack.

By 6:30 in the morning, they must leave the shelter, taking all their belongings with them. Preschool children are accompanied by their mothers to the children's day care shelter across town. Once there, they wait in a parking lot hoping to get a space inside. The shelter serves only 30 children and admittance is on a first-come, first-served basis.

The 30 children at the front of the line spend the rest of the day at the shelter. Their mothers may not stay with them. There is simply no room.

Small children, therefore, are left in a strange place with strangers. They are safe and warm, but they are away from their mothers. Those children turned away from the shelter spend their day either wandering the streets with their mothers or accompanying their mothers to job interviews, social service appointments or sitting idly in a women's day shelter. Even tiny tots must help their mothers carry their belongings around town until the night shelter opens at 7:00 p.m. Often as a kindness, the police transport the children from one shelter to another. Eating a meal is not something that is guaranteed. These children do not engage in American life. They only observe it passing them by. They are the watchers.

School-aged children leave the shelter at 6:30 in the morning. They walk to the nearest school bus stop where they wait perhaps two hours on the street corners, unsupervised, and often in the dark. Knowing that they may not remain in a particular school, they often deliberately avoid social interaction and involvement in school activities. They hope for anonymity. They don't want to be identified as being homeless.

When the school day ends, they return to the same bus stop to watch their peers go home. They must at all cost avoid anyone knowing that they live at a shelter.

From 3:30 to 7:00 p.m. when the night shelter opens, they have to find a way to be safe. They wait for a turn to be an ordinary child. Occasionally, police again will transport them from one shelter to another.

About 5:30 p.m., families begin to meet at predetermined places to begin the process of finding a shelter for the night. Finally, after 14 hours of carrying and guarding their belongings, these families can rest. In large public spaces, they group themselves as families. In public bathrooms, they wash themselves and their clothes, taking turns and hoping for a moment of family life. Mothers sleep with their children on mats and cots on gymnasium floors. Children — homeless children — live in public spaces 24 hours a day and wait for a home.

Homeless children do not find the world a wondrous place for joyful discovery. Homeless children are the waiters and the watchers.

Among the findings in the research conducted by Anita Beaty of the Atlanta Task Force For the Homeless and myself are a couple that I'd like to share with you that capture their experience.

One theme is that the children have an intense desire to proclaim their own self worth. The children resist adult attempts to clump them into categories of deprived, poor or pitiful children.

Debra, an eight-year-old, was in the kitchen with me cleaning up after we served dinner to the persons in the shelter. She asked me if she could have a job to do. So I gave her a job. She said to me, "I'm finished, Nancy, give me another job." So I gave her a second job to do. I gave her a third job to do. She announced that she was all done, and I praised her warmly and told her that I was sure her mother was very pleased to have such a good helper in the family. She said, "Will you give me something for doing my jobs?"

I said, "No, I have nothing to give you." Quite seriously she said, "Yes, yes, you do." My mind anticipated a request for money or dessert. I asked, "What do I have to give?"

She said, "You can give me a hug. You can always give a hug when you have nothing else to give."

Kevin, age 6, asserted himself in a different way. He entered the kitchen forcefully and clearly requested more food from the volunteers.

With pride and manners, he said, "May I have seconds? But don't give me any of that chicken. I don't like it. I want the other meat."

What I heard and saw was his refusal to allow nameless adults to describe his world. I watched him feeling confident about his ability to discriminate and to be known by his likes and dislikes.

There are many ways in which the children of all ages continually find to say who they are. For most children in the shelter, tomorrow is a fuzzy and ambiguous prospect. There is only the certainty of the morning routine of leaving the shelter. The remainder of the day is not assured. Among themselves, the children speak about being different from other children. They know that they acquire the basic things of life in ways that are different from other children.

Nothing, no part of their day, is predictable. They live in a gap of uncertainty.

The final example is Keisha, who is 9 and who expressed a profound ambivalence about her place in the world. She hung herself around my neck and back, asking me how many children I had. I said, "None." "Oh," she said. "My mom says that people who don't have children are blessed." Not believing my ears, I said, "She's right, it is a blessing to have children." With firmness, Keisha said, "No, she said people who *don't* have children are blessed." Her whole body asked me what I thought. I felt her question deep on my insides. Much later in the evening, before I left the shelter, I found Keisha and told her that I was sure that meeting her was a blessing in my life.

Our findings show that these children are over-anxious, sad, angry, lonely, depressed, frustrated and cautious. They are at high risk to succumb to the scourges of poverty. Their behavior is reflective of and congruent with their circumstances. Their behavior is out of order because their lives are out of order.

The Atlanta Task Force for the Homeless, the Phyliss Wheatly YMCA, the Junior League and other agencies and organizations are doing what they can, but the efforts of a few cannot possibly solve a systematic problem.

I believe that the way one forms a question, Mr. Chairman, prescribes the answer. I have begun to call homeless children the waiters and the watchers. They are waiting and watching us, depending upon the answers.

Ella Mae Wade Brayboy

Ella Mae Wade Brayboy is a longtime community activist in Atlanta, best known for her work with voter registration. Immediately before retiring in 1995, she worked as the Community Outreach Coordinator for the Martin Luther King Jr. Center for Nonviolent Social Change.

Brayboy has worked with voter registration since 1962 with the All Citizen Registration Committee and the Voter Education Project, sponsored by the Southern Christian Leadership Conference. She was one of the first black deputy registrars in Atlanta and helped place voter registration in the Atlanta Public Library System. She has served on numerous boards, including Wesley Homes and Ebenezer Baptist Church Day Care Center for the Elderly. She is currently a member of the Fulton County Council on Aging and assists elderly persons applying for benefits.

Brayboy is the widow of William Brayboy; she has three daughters, seven grandchildren and three great-grandchildren.

TAX RELIEF FOR SENIOR CITIZENS
Ella Mae Brayboy to the Fulton County Board of Commissioners
Atlanta — February, 2000

I have come today to speak in support of an amendment that would waive unpaid and delinquent taxes, penalties, and interest for individuals 65 years and older with incomes less than $39,000. I ask you to remember the sacrifices made by your parents and grandparents in purchasing homes, through some of the most financially stressful periods of their lives. Fifty, even 60 years ago, today's seniors were young individuals who made sacrifices in saving up for a down payment on a home. Today, almost 8,000 seniors are experiencing difficulty in paying taxes, and 4,000 are considered as delinquent. These are the same ones who faithfully paid property taxes for 40, 50, 60 years.

Do you question seniors who have been consistent for this time and become delinquent in old age? It's because many do not have the income or the family support or, in some cases, the health or strength to manage their daily business needs. This is a very emotional issue because the common thread found in my generation is knowing the privilege of the vote and knowing the value of purchasing a home — the vote because blacks and women were denied the privilege and the home because of the struggles my generation experienced meeting monthly notes.

Many elderly homeowners were a generation of service workers who worked for sometimes $5 a week. One stated that you were not paid by cash but by money that came out of the employer's pocket. This is a generation who struggled to purchase homes that may now be valued at $45,000. For many poor seniors, they are property rich with empty pocketbooks. Most of the poorest live on incomes of less than $500 per month because they worked during an era when there were no payments made into the Social Security system, no minimum wages and no down-payment assistance program.

Therefore, the aging community is appalled when we understand that these same homes are lost because of delinquent property taxes.

Senior citizen advocates of Fulton County are seeking your support in including this amendment in the legislative package. We commend Commissioner Darnell for her leadership in feeling the pulse of the community, and we commend you for your support in this critical issue. Thank you.

Anna R. Cablik

Anna R. Cablik is the founder of Anatek Inc., a contracting company specializing in highway bridges, and Anasteel & Supply Company, the only Hispanic and female-owned reinforcing steel fabricator in the Southeast.

Cablik is currently on the board of the United Way and is the co-chair of membership for the Georgia Chamber of Commerce. She is past chair of the board of the Atlanta Hispanic Chamber of Commerce and has served on the boards of the Latin American Association, Saint Joseph's Mercy Care and the Fulton Atlanta Community Action Authority. She also works with other Hispanic entrepreneurs to assist them in starting businesses.

Cablik was born and raised in the Republic of Panama. She came to Atlanta in 1974 with her husband, Jerry Cablik. They have three sons, Alan, Kevin and Ryan.

INDIVIDUAL RESPONSIBILITY

Anna Cablik to the Leadership Atlanta Class (Excerpts)

Atlanta — June, 2000

*S*trength or force exerted or capable of being exerted; might. Ability or official capacity to exercise control; authority.

These are the definitions that usually come to mind when I think of the word *power*. I do not believe that I have much authority and even less might. However, the first definition of power in my dictionary is the ability or capacity to act or perform effectively. Using this definition, and applying it to my businesses, I can accept that I am a woman of certain power.

I am a successful business woman. I own and control two businesses, and just for the record, my husband has absolutely nothing to do with these businesses. And if I would have to choose just one critical issue to improve life in Atlanta, I would call it individual responsibility.

But today I will talk about four critical issues: education, business, politics and media within the framework of individual responsibility.

The first critical issue that must be considered is education. In order to have a good education, we cannot continue to point fingers at each other. We cannot always blame someone else. In order to have a good education, every one of us needs to be involved from a personal standpoint.

To have a good education, every parent needs to believe that education is important. Every child needs to understand that with education, he will have a better future. Every teacher needs to conscientiously work, believing that the education that he or she provides is the most important thing there could be. The politicians need to believe in education; each business person needs to believe in education.

But it is not good enough simply to believe in education; it is necessary to do something. To blame the teachers, the children or the parents does not accomplish anything. If each one of us takes our piece and does what it takes, things will improve and quickly. I believe that if parents are constantly vigilant of what is going on at school, children can get a good education in any school system. Maybe you need to get involved in mentoring a child, maybe you need to get involved in politics to put pressure on the different governmental entities to improve the school system, although improving the school system does not mean building new schools. The quality of the education has nothing to do with a building. It has a lot more to do with what a teacher knows and how they can pass that information. In many instances, the success of a school system is directly correlated to how much involvement there is from the parents. Some of these parents are workers, some are business owners, some are just parents, but all have a role to play.

The second issue is individual responsibility in business. The business community has a lot of influence in what goes on in Atlanta. And businesses can improve the life of a community in many ways. By using your influence with your coworkers and employees, you can push the envelope for better education.

Even though diversity in the workplace is a very commonly used phrase these days, I am not convinced that it is a reality. Words and clichés do not accomplish anything. Action is what counts; valuing each employee for their work, regardless of their looks or their accents.

Every one of us has our prejudices. We need to set those aside and look at things more objectively. Most individuals are looking for the same thing: a safe home for themselves and their family, a good education for the children and a better future. If we take time to get to know people from different backgrounds, soon we will find out that we are not that different. Yes, there are cultural differences; I acknowledge them and do not consider them a negative. Most people feel more comfortable when they are among people of their own culture and background. But that should not mean that in the workplace we cannot mingle and work together.

The third critical issue is individual responsibility in politics. Coming from a country where politics is a dirty word and where respectable citizens stay as far away from politics as they can, it was a great disappointment to find out that the political process is not that honorable here either. To my shock, I have found politicians who, in my opinion, are politicians because they could not find a "real job." It has appalled me to have politicians approach me for their support and, when asked what their platform or agenda was, I was told that it did not matter; they were the only Hispanic running for that particular office. It is sad that a politician would have that attitude, but what is even worse is that voters actually buy this garbage. We need qualified politicians. It is our responsibility as citizens to learn what the real issues are, to analyze each candidate's proposal. Our quality of politicians would improve dramatically if we as voters would expect it and demand it. And this brings me to my last critical issue: the media.

How could the media improve the life of Atlanta? Probably the best way for the media to improve the life in Atlanta is to report the facts, both the good and the bad. The job of the media is to report facts, not to report their opinion.

Why can't the media publish more positive occurrences instead of wearing us all out with all the negative? I am not saying they should not report the negatives; obviously, if they are factual, they should be reported. But why is it that the media will report over and over when a college fraternity member gets killed because of crazy and ridiculous rituals they engage in, but they do not report the philanthropic and community service provided by fraternities? Why is it not published that in most instances, fraternity brothers do have better grades than the rest of the students?

What can we do about this? Take personal responsibility. If you are a reporter, journalist or newscaster, report the facts. If you are a consumer of the media, don't buy it until there is more responsible reporting facts.

Power: the ability or capacity to act or perform effectively.

Four critical issues: education, business, politics and media within the framework of individual responsibility.

I hope you will join me in recognizing your own power and accepting your individual responsibility in each of these areas of life.

Pin Pin Chau

Pin Pin Chau is the CEO of Summit Bank Corporation, the holding company for Summit National Bank. Summit is based in Atlanta with offices in Atlanta and San Jose, California. The bank focuses on small business, international trade and ethnic community banking.

Chau was born in Hong Kong and came to the United States as an undergraduate student. She serves on the board of directors of the Atlanta College of Arts, Consumer Credit Counseling Service and the Carter Center Board of Councilors. Appointed by Governor Roy Barnes to the board of the Georgia Department of Industry, Trade and Tourism, she serves on the Executive Committee. She is a graduate of Leadership Atlanta and a member of the International Women's Forum and the Society of International Business Fellows.

Chau is married to Dr. Raymond Chau; they have one grown daughter, Christine.

LEADERSHIP AT ITS BEST

Pin Pin Chau to the Priority Associates Luncheon

Atlanta — April, 2000

If I tell you today that you will have the opportunity to wear a yellow jacket, ride a horse up Pennsylvania Avenue and be given a peacock feather for your cap when you arrive at the White House, you would probably ask me what kind of practical joke is this? Now, imagine that you lived in Imperial China a hundred years ago. You would have died a thousand deaths, and indeed, thousands of young men would have already died on your behalf for that distinct honor. Chinese history tells us that it was exactly what the emperor did for the most outstanding general in 300 years of the Ching Dynasty — being able to wear the imperial color, not having to dismount and kneel all the way through the imperial grounds to the throne-room, and being awarded the most distinguished badge of honor, one feather of an auspicious imperial bird.

The point is: While customs differ and symbols of achievement may change with time and culture, it is a part of human consciousness to be challenged to be the best one can be and to connect to that which one considers worthwhile. On one hand, there is success, which is often measured by concrete possessions and privileges. On the other, there is a yearning to be outstanding, often measured by intellectual capacity or fame. Furthermore, there is a desire to be remembered beyond one's lifetime, measured by what is called legacy.

If we are really honest about it, at one time or another in our lives, we fall for one or the other or all of the above. Sometimes, we can be quite foolish going about it. When I was very young, before I even started kindergarten, someone told me this Chinese proverb: *If you can handle suffering and bitterness, you can be a superior human being.*

I ate a lot of bitter melons (it's a very bitter, ugly-looking vegetable that only the Chinese and Asian Indians have acquired a taste for), and I offered to eat them uncooked to get the full intensity of bitterness. In my naiveté, I thought that handling suffering and bitterness was to eat something bitter that I didn't like whatsoever; I fell for the Chinese version of Popeye and spinach. As a teenager (that impossible age of budding self-awareness without self-knowledge), in typical teenage sense of melancholy, I thought that life was so transient that unless I left a footprint in history, I would be forgotten, just like a grain of sand on the human shore. The desire to expand my horizon eventually gave me courage to leave my mainstream world to be a minority person in America shortly after high school.

> *If you can handle suffering and bitterness,*
> *you can be a superior human being.*
> — Chinese Proverb

Why is the striving for fortune, fame and legacy so prevalent in human beings? I submit that we are wired for the survival of us as human beings. Possession and privileges appeal to the survival instinct to take care of our body. Fame satisfies our emotion and intellect, what some would call our soul. Leaving a legacy is striving to survive our finite and transient life to connect to eternity, the aspiration of our spirit.

There is no end of fads and fetishes we go through to perfect our body, or at least, at my stage of life, to delay the inevitable total capitulation in the battle of the bulges — without sacrificing dessert. I received an email this morning from one of my colleagues. The message reads: "Pin Pin, I do believe you will like this one," accompanied by a smiley face. The attachment is a chubby little kitten with her eyes closed in perfect attention and the heading reads: "Please God. If you can't make me thin, make my friends fat!" Talk about teamwork and bearing each other's burden! We really do not need to dwell too much on the physical aspect of our existence and how some people can accumulate more possessions and privileges. There are bells and whistles to warn us if we do not take care of our body, at least on a minimal basis.

The world's great literature, art and scientific discoveries attest to the power of the human soul and, on a more personal basis, a soul mate relationship is an emotion concrete enough to touch. There are other ways to please our soul. For us in the financial profession, how about that corner office on the 56th floor and the power that goes with it? Some of us women are not really comfortable with the word power because we conjure up negative things about it. Surely, power without leadership is dangerous. Power is self-focused while leadership is empowering others to be the best they can be — along a shared vision. So it is important that we examine ourselves and are satisfied with how power is obtained, exercised and for what purpose.

There is no end of fads and fetishes we go through to perfect our body, or at least, at my stage of life, to delay the inevitable total capitulation in the battle of the bulges — without sacrificing dessert.

Thus, leadership at one level is concrete. It must provide visible results or quantifiable differences in this physical world that we occupy. A good leader must be able to mobilize resources to empower the constituent towards the common good. On another level, good leadership must be able to inspire our souls, be that intellectual or emotional. A good leader discerns our hopes and dreams and knows our fears. A good leader is, therefore, addicted to life-long learning and growth so that he or she knows how to take acceptable risks to achieve our goals and to allay our fears, because change is not a total stranger to those who keep up with the times. We like to say that some people are lucky, but often luck is when preparation meets opportunity.

Those leadership qualities pertaining to the body and soul aspects of our human nature are probably very self-evident. But leadership at its best needs to be rooted in integrity and spiritual strength, which is not so evident until one is awakened by that still small voice. Leadership at its best is confident and secure. It is authentic and not paranoid. It is decent and honest. It is found in a personal relationship with God — the God who reached out to mankind in history, who continues to reach out in every present day through the love letter He left for us — the *Bible* — and in the reality of His presence in those who walk with Him.

If I offend your sensitivity by being so direct, please do not blame your friend who invited you because this is my personal belief and I cannot omit this last factor. Forgive me for being personal about this, because the relationship He has with each one who seeks and answers His call is personal.

Leadership at its best needs to be rooted in integrity and spiritual strength, which is not so evident until one is awakened by that still small voice. Leadership at its best is confident and secure. It is authentic and not paranoid. It is decent and honest.

This personal relationship is my connection to eternity here and now. It gives me assurance of my status as a human being, not based upon what others think of me, or worse still, my own critical evaluation of myself. It is important to me that His love is unconditional and He values me enough to have my name inscribed in the palm of His hand as He stated in the Book of Isaiah. It feels good to know that I am OK, even if I am not perfect and even if every decision I have to make is not going to please everyone.

My confidence is not based on trusting in myself, since I know my own limitations the best. I trust in a higher power who has never failed me, a power who would rather that I open wide to receive freely what He is willing to give, because giving does not diminish Him. Knowing this gives me tremendous security about myself, my work and my relationship with others. I do not need to be armored and invincible. I can be vulnerable without being defeated. I can be authentic yet principled. I can trust and be trusted. There can be no leadership without trust.

I do not limit God and, therefore, no one can define my perimeters, not even myself. I can say, "I can."

In conclusion, let me draw your attention to my favorite toy, the kaleidoscope. Are there some of you who share the same interest? I discovered why it pleases us, because it appeals to both sides of our brain. The enjoyment it gives is the element of surprise at every turn — exciting and creative color and new designs — but you can also count on it to be structured and symmetrical.

I took a class at the Spruill Center for the Arts to learn to make a kaleidoscope and found out that the symmetry is provided by three mirrors forming a perfect triangle and the surprise element is provided by a random assortment of colorful glass bits.

Leadership at its best is like a kaleidoscope. Body, soul and spirit, fully synchronized, provide the structure so that there is room for creativity and for the unexpected events of life to fall in their right places. There is beauty and wisdom in the structure and joy in the journey. Let me wish you joy in the journey as you and I continue to refine our structure and balance in our triune being.

Pearl Cleage

Pearl Cleage is an Atlanta-based writer whose works include novels, plays, essays and articles. Her novel, *What Looks Like Crazy On An Ordinary Day,* was an Oprah Book Club pick and appeared on the *New York Times* bestseller list for nine weeks. Her later novel, *I Wish I Had A Red Dress*, was published in July 2001.

Cleage's recent theatrical works include *Bourbon at the Border, Flyin' West* and *Blues for An Alabama Sky*, all of which premiered at The Alliance Theatre in Atlanta under the direction of Kenny Leon. Her collection of essays, *Deals with the Devil and Other Reasons to Riot*, was published in 1993. She is a former columnist for the *Atlanta Tribune,* and her articles have appeared in many publications, including *Essence Magazine, Ms.* and *Vibe.*

Cleage is the mother of one daughter, Deignan, and is the wife of Zaron W. Burnett Jr.

DREAMING OF CAMPFIRES
Pearl Cleage to the Women's Resource Center Luncheon
Atlanta — April, 2000

Imagine it is dinnertime. Imagine we are sitting around a campfire. We are ancient, magical women who live in peace with all creatures so that just beyond our cooking circle, the lions that we keep around as allies more than pets are yawning and settling their massive heads on their massive paws while we confer and confess, conducting our business as ancient, magical women often do over steaming pots and sleeping children, a stone's throw from the mysterious male creatures with whom we share our blankets and our babies and our blood memories.

Imagine our business includes culture and commerce and healthcare and technology and defense and diversions and endless discussions of what it means to fall in love and stay here. Imagine there is a full moon. Imagine there is peace and plenty and safety and spirit. Imagine what language we might speak. Imagine the sound of our laughter...

I have been dreaming of campfires. Women spaces where we can talk uninterrupted; where the only requirements are love, peace and the truth, the whole truth and nothing but the truth.

My sisters and my friends, I want us to gather here as if in the safety of our campfire and admit to each other that we are in crisis. I want us to admit that the problem of violence against women is growing, despite our best efforts, and now manifests itself in Atlanta in the person of a small army of child prostitutes, working our streets from dusk until dawn as regularly as they would if they were taking orders at McDonald's. I want to talk about these girls — our girls — because I think their exploitation is the most virulent form of domestic violence, child abuse and overall male madness.

I am here to help us keep them uppermost in our minds because it is so easy to get distracted. Because they have already faded from the front pages of the daily paper, their stories already old news, their pictures crowded out by spy planes and race riots and televised executions sanctioned by the attorney general's office, as if killing one person can ever bring peace to another. Already the phrase, "10-year-old prostitute," has faded away, its power so diminished that it no longer makes us cringe, or cry, and it should. It must.

Remember when you were 10? I do. I didn't have breasts yet. I hadn't had a period yet. I had never kissed anybody who wasn't related to me by blood or bond, and whose kiss carried only a message of love and tenderness, and caring, peace and protection. I had never had a sexual thought. I had never been touched in a sexual way. The only penises I had ever seen belonged to my cousin Warren when we were three and still took our baths together, and to my startled father, who stepped out of the shower one afternoon to find me waiting with a question or a curiosity. I don't remember which. What I remember is he calmly put on his robe and shooed me out until he could get dressed, which is what a father is supposed to do.

I remember being 10. I played with my dolls, jumped rope, roller-skated and walked the three blocks to the playground with my sister. I made angels in the snow and set the table at my grandmomma's house for Sunday dinner and hung a stocking at Christmas time. I went to church with my daddy and learned how to sew from my mama, fell asleep in the backseat on the way home from wherever because it was late and I was tired, and I knew somebody would carry me inside, tuck me in, kiss me goodnight and make sure nothing bad happened to me because that's what families do for their baby girls, isn't it? Because that's what being a little black girl is all about, isn't it?

See, I remember being 10. That's part of why I'm here today. I am a sister, a daughter, a mother, a wife and a free woman, and I thought I might have something helpful to say. I thought I might be able to put things into perspective; to state things more clearly; to help us focus our thoughts and our energies and our resources on ways to address the terrible problem at hand, but I was wrong.

I don't know what to say about our sons prostituting our daughters. I don't know what to say about 10-year-old girls having sex for money because they are in fear for their lives and nobody seems to know what to do with them. How many studies do we need to know that prostituting a child is an act of war against all women? It is an act of such violence and cruelty and insanity that the perpetrators seem to me to be something other than my brothers ... something new and strange and terrible and frightening. Something that demands a new analysis, a new articulation and a new approach.

Nothing we know is working. None of the protections we are used to thinking about are in place. These baby girls are alone in the world, at the mercy of male human beings who have the nerve to call themselves men, but whom we must call by their real name of *pimp* ... by their real name of *predator*.

They are not our brothers. Brothers do not rape their sisters, their children and their babies. Who are they, these men? Who are they, now sleeping so close to us, close enough to endanger our children? Who are they and what is the proper response to their presence among us?

It is a terrible question, isn't it? But remember, we're talking about being 10-years-old here. We're talking about doll babies and jungle gyms and flannel pajamas, but that's just a corny dream when you're wearing your high-heeled shoes and your little pink bra and your tight little skirt, switching your little 10-year-old child's behind down Metropolitan Parkway. And all we read about, hear about and are supposed to think about is how many spies are returning home in triumph and how much money it takes to be elected mayor of Atlanta.

I'm tired of talking about that. I'm tired of talking about infrastructure and water rights and who's moving into the city and who's moving out. I want to talk about what kind of man decides to make a living by selling the bodies of 10-year-old girls from cheap motel rooms. I want to talk about why all those progressive politicians we keep electing to look out for our interests can't find the money right now, today, to open the best treatment facility in the country right here to save our baby girls. We know what we need, so why don't we do it?

The terrible truth is because, as a city, we don't care. These are invisible children just like the murdered ghosts who once put Atlanta on the map as a place that couldn't protect its children and we all swore it would never happen again. But it is happening right now, every day and every night. How can that be?

It is because these are poor little black girls. Little black baby girls with absent fathers and damaged mothers, or exhausted grandparents and at-their-wits-end caregivers. It is because we don't have to see them as long as we never go south of downtown and keep our eyes fixed firmly on the nightclub district, the new state flag, the pollen count, our World Series chances and the possibility of tee-ball games on the south White House lawn.

But I want to talk about being 10-years-old. I want to talk about having a daddy who doesn't love me and a mamma who is so damaged she can't take care of me. I want to talk about being kidnapped and beaten and terrorized and prostituted. I want to talk about what it feels like to be forced to have sex with men old enough to be my daddy, 10 times a day, without a condom, without a bath and without birth control.

I want to talk about the pimps, even though I know we changed the law. We at least had the power to change the law, but the law is only useful after the crime has been committed. I want to address the more difficult question of prevention. I want to address the question of protection. I want to address the question of how we have come to the place where the most present, visible enemy of too many women and children in Atlanta, in 2001, is the men who are prepared to destroy them for cash, cars, clothes and the admiration of other men who share their cruel madness.

Now tell me I'm wrong. Please, tell me I'm wrong. I want to be wrong, but this is our campfire, right? And my grandmother said truth is the light, so denying the reality of what we are seeing means we will never identify the problem and, therefore, never find the solution. And while we're running from the difficulty of the question, a generation of little black girls is being destroyed right under our noses, right in the shadow of all those skyscrapers. How can we let that happen?

We can't. Our babies are suffering the atrocities of war, and we cannot allow the polite municipal dialogue to continue without making those atrocities the center of every political discussion that takes place in our town. We must demand not talk, but action, from every level of elected official. We must require of our sisters and brothers who are running for political office, from the mayor on down, that they stand with us on this issue by making it the center of their campaigns. Not because they are good managers, or good politicians, or good fundraisers, but because they are good mothers and loving fathers. And if that was their little girl baby out there walking down Metropolitan Parkway in her little fake leather skirt and high-heeled shoes, offering to have any kind of sex you can think of for five dollars, there would be no question that there would be headlines and campaigns and money to do the work that needs to be done.

So that is our job as a community. We have to change the discussion, the focus, the priorities. We have to be prepared to write letters and have demonstrations, hold vigils and organize picket lines the way women do all over the world when their families are threatened. We have to walk as if we were in Pinochet's Chile holding up the photos of our missing relatives. We have to talk as if we were in the South Africa of old, honoring a long-jailed Nelson Mandela by continuing his dedication to the freedom struggle until he can rejoin us. It is time for us to stand up as women, as mothers have done all over the world. And while we must welcome the help of the men we trust, we must also admit that many of the men we have trusted to lead us have failed and abandoned us. They have focused on the wrong things for the wrong reasons, and we have only to look around us to see the results of their inattention. What good is a new stadium, if in its shadow 10-year-old babies are being sold into sexual slavery? Who cares if Puff Daddy goes free and Michael Jordan might play basketball again or we finally elect a woman to the mayor's office if we still can't watch our little girls grow into their womanhood strong, safe and free?

I have been dreaming of campfires. I have been dreaming of a city we can feel safe in, a city we can feel proud of, a city where women finally take the leadership and the responsibility in the struggle to save ourselves and save our children … because that's what we're supposed to do, because we already have the power if we will only recognize it, embrace it and use it. Because being 10 isn't about selling your soul; it's about learning how to dream.

Brenda Hill Cole

Brenda Hill Cole is a state court judge of Fulton County, having been appointed by Governor Zell Miller in 1998.

Cole is a member of the boards of the Atlanta Women's Foundation, *Women Looking Ahead* news magazine and the Michael C. Carlos Museum of Emory University. She also serves on the board of the Council of State Court Judges and is a member of the Lawyer's Club of Atlanta, the Atlanta Bar Association, the Georgia Association of Women Lawyers and the National Bar Association.

Cole is also the founder of the Clark Atlanta University Guild, an organization that provides scholarships for arts and humanities students at Clark Atlanta University.

Cole is married to Dr. Thomas W. Cole Jr., president of Clark Atlanta University. They are the parents of Kelley Susann and Thomas III.

CELEBRATING THE ACCOMPLISHMENTS OF WOMEN
*Brenda Cole to the Charleston Institute Chapter of Links Inc.,
Women's History Month Program*
Charleston, West Virginia — May, 1999

May has been set aside as Women's History Month and it is appropriate that we take note of the accomplishments of women over the years. Sometimes we get so busy that we don't take the time to stop and reflect on where we've come from and the people who paved the way. In the book of Jeremiah, chapter 6, verse 16 reads: *"Stand at the crossroads and look, and ask for the ancient paths, where the good way lies and walk in it, and find rest for your souls."*

Knowing our history is so important. We all need to stand and reflect on the roads we've traveled, the victories and defeats. What better way to determine if we're on the right path for the destination we have chosen? History not only provides knowledge of where we've been, but a road map, a guide to the future and inspiration for the travel. If our ancestors achieved so much under such trying circumstances, surely we can overcome many of the problems facing our generation. If we concentrate only on the present, we may see the glass as half empty. Too often, the news is not good: low economic status of female-headed households, reduced opportunities for advancement because of the "glass ceiling," increased teenage pregnancy, increased incidences of domestic violence and other crimes against women. We all need to know our history. Then, we can see the progress we've made and provide encouragement for young girls traveling the road ahead.

Women have always been leaders — in homes, churches, schools and businesses. In biblical times, women such as Esther were brave and assertive. In 1695, Queen Anne was the first female chief of a Native American tribe. Women were key to the settlement and growth of this country. But for much of history, women were expected to play a supportive role, a subservient role, not a leadership role. In 1848, the Women's Rights Convention was held in Seneca Falls, New York, where the Declaration of Sentiments was produced. It was patterned after the

Declaration of Independence and called for equal rights for women. From 1854 until 1860, Susan B. Anthony crusaded for women's rights in the United States and worldwide. It was not until 1920 that women in the United States got the right to vote with the passage of the 19th Amendment. It was not until 1965, with the passage of the Voting Rights Act, that black Americans secured the right to go to the polls.

We've come a long way since Susan B. Anthony began her fight for women's rights. Ms. Anthony would not have dreamed that within 150 years of her movement, women would serve as prime ministers of India, New Zealand, Canada, Turkey, Pakistan, Great Britain and Israel; presidents of Ireland (twice), Guyana and the Philippines. She may not have dreamed that today in the United States, women would sit on the U.S. Supreme Court, serve in the House and Senate of the United States and in many states. A woman's place is not only in the home, but in the House, the Senate and yes, some day, the White House. The first step in opening doors for women is in understanding that we are entitled and our daughters are entitled to do anything we have the brains, energy and desire to do.

In 1996, women owned one-third of all U.S. businesses, employing 26 percent of the nation's work force. Sales from the 7.95 million

Women have always been leaders – in homes, churches, schools and businesses.

women-owned businesses jumped 236 percent since 1987 and employment rose to 18.5 million workers. According to the National Foundation for Women Business Owners, the number of women-owned companies increased 78 percent from 1986 through 1995, while growth among other U.S. firms was only 47 percent.

Law schools are reporting dramatic increases in the numbers of women graduates, in some cases over 60 percent. In 1977, when I graduated from law school, there were no women or blacks on the state and superior courts in Fulton County, Georgia. Now, of the nine state court judges, there are four women, three of whom are black. On the superior court, there are 17 judges; 10 are women, four of whom are black. Women in law and government have made progress in the Georgia Legislature. Of the 56 senators, 10 are women (five black); of the 180 representatives, 35 are women (11 black).

We salute these outstanding women and their predecessors who paved the way. When I was a young girl, there were no women lawyers

> *A woman's place is not only in the home, but in the House, the Senate and yes, some day, the White House. The first step in opening doors for women is in understanding that we are entitled and our daughters are entitled to do anything we have the brains, energy and desire to do.*

or judges in the small Texas town where I grew up. I never aspired to be a lawyer or judge because I was not aware that it was within the realm of possibility. Recognizing our heroes is very important because of the inspiration it provides to our youth.

Mrs. Mary McLeod Bethune was a hero who blazed new trails for women. She was an educator who founded Bethune-Cookman College. She was a champion of humanitarian and democratic values throughout the United States. Mrs. Bethune provided the leadership to raise black women from the social and political invisibility they suffered to an important presence in national affairs. She challenged women to stop playing bridge and start building bridges.

I didn't know about black women lawyers until I heard about Judge Constance Baker Motley, a brilliant and path-breaking civil rights lawyer who became America's first black female federal judge. She was formerly a New York state senator and Manhattan borough president. Judge Motley joined Thurgood Marshall's legal team at the NAACP legal defense and educational fund in 1945, at a time when women lawyers were uncommon and black women lawyers even more uncommon. Judge Motley was chief counsel for James Meredith in his legal fight to be the first black to attend the University of Mississippi and represented other leading civil rights and women's rights leaders. Constance Baker Motley is a hero.

An unlikely hero is Miss Osceola McCarty, a laundry woman from Mississippi who stopped school in the sixth grade to take care of an invalid aunt. She never married or had children. She spent her life washing and ironing for others. Because of her frugal lifestyle, she never had a car or a color TV. She saved $250,000, which she used for her church and for scholarships to the University of Southern Mississippi for needy black students in her hometown. Miss McCarty will always be remembered for her sacrifice to help the next generation and her generosity of spirit.

It is important to understand that there are always those persons who don't want women to advance, and each of us has a part to play to see that the progress for women continues. One way to do that is by highlighting the contributions of women who have made a difference.

> *When I was a young girl, there were no women lawyers or judges in the small Texas town where I grew up. I never aspired to be a lawyer or judge because I was not aware that it was within the realm of possibility.*

Some have compared life to a relay race, where each generation has its turn to grasp the baton. Many outstanding women who came before us have run a great race and passed the baton to us, but they were not destined to see the race to the finish. We also may not see the goal of true equality for women, but we must be ready for the hand-off from our ancestors.

We must be prepared and trained just as competitive athletes. You can't just show up at the race without preparation and expect to win.

Grasp the baton firmly, with determination, realizing the sacrifices that were made so that we might have an opportunity. It is important that we don't drop the baton, don't let the doors of opportunity that were opened for us close on our watch. Then, we must run as best we can to gain new ground in order to pass the baton to a new generation. "Stand at the crossroads and look, and ask for the ancient paths, where the good way lies, and walk in it, and find rest for your souls."

Johnnetta B. Cole

Dr. Johnnetta B. Cole is president emerita of Spelman College, having become the first African-American woman to serve as president of the college in 1987. She is also professor emerita of Emory University, from which she recently retired as Presidential Distinguished Professor of Anthropology, Women's Studies and African-American Studies.

Cole is a member of The Links Inc. and the National Council of Negro Women. She serves on the board of directors of Coca-Cola Enterprises and Merck & Co. Inc., and is a trustee of Gallaudet University and the Rockefeller Foundation. Since retiring from university teaching and administration, she continues writing, speaking, consulting and engaging in community service.

Cole is married to Arthur J. Robinson Jr. and has three sons, two stepsons and two grandchildren.

WOMEN IN THE NEW CENTURY: A CALL TO LEADERSHIP
Johnnetta B. Cole to the faculty, students and friends of Mills College
(Excerpts)
Birmingham, Alabama — September, 1999

As a nation, we will never reach our full potential until we draw on the talents, sensitivities, perspectives and just plain smarts of all of our people. There is a Chinese saying that captures this idea of the necessity of diversity, the strength in having all of our nation's people engaged and involved, the beauty of full participation. The saying is this: *One flower never makes a spring!*

Indeed, we *womenfolks* are a magnificent "spring," reflecting a stunning expression of colors, conditions, circumstances and choices.

Imagine what a country we would have if difference didn't make any difference. Imagine if people of different races, genders, sexual orientations, ages, religions and physical abilities were viewed as just plain folks! I want to share with you another saying. The origin of it is not certain, but many say that it is of American Indian origin. For certain, it belongs to all of us. The saying is this: *Women Hold Up Half the Sky.* And indeed we do.

While there is a tremendous amount of diversity among womenfolks – if you have seen one of us, you haven't seen us all – we also share so very, very much. After all, it is we who are assumed to be incapable of over-performing complicated tasks as well as a man – complicated tasks like driving a car. It is we who, when we are in a domestic arrangement with a man, are often assumed to have been born with a special device in our heads that allows us to locate missing objects – and thus, a husband continues to ask his wife, "Where are my socks?"

More seriously, it is we womenfolks who are assumed to be in charge of raising the next generation and caring for the one that preceded us. It is we women who, on the average, are paid only 78 cents for the one dollar men earn doing the same jobs. It is we women who, far more than men, are the victims of the most brutalizing violence there is – rape.

But it is also we women who can know the joy of literally giving birth to another human being; and it is we women who can experience the exquisite pleasures of sisterhood.

> *Each time the first woman is appointed to some position, it is indeed a victory to be celebrated. It is also a reminder of how much work is yet to be done.*

I want to turn now to some comments about women and leadership. Until very recently, whenever someone drew a picture of a leader, imagined a leader of this or that, portrayed a leader in a magazine or newspaper or on television, the most frequent image — indeed, it seemed like the only images — were men. And over and over and over again, the men were white.

As we move into the next century, when we womenfolks and people of color will be a numerical majority, can it and will it remain that way? I don't think so. In raising the question of women as leaders, one wonders what we might learn from studying and, where appropriate, adapting to our needs different styles of leadership. Imagine what it might be like if there were new ways of leading, being carried out by a new kind of leader in a new century.

A possible source of models for us is international women leaders. From places like India, Nigeria, Afghanistan, Ireland, Israel, Barbados, the Philippines and South Africa, there is much that we can learn about how women serve as leaders in both formal and informal ways. Surely there is much that we can learn from our sisters throughout the global village.

Over the past few years, here in our nation, we have seen an unprecedented number of American women assume leadership positions as school superintendents, judges and university presidents. Today, women are more often acknowledged as leaders in Congress, in corporations and in an array of organizations.

Each time the first woman is appointed to some position, it is indeed a victory to be celebrated. It is also a reminder of how much work is yet to be done. There are so many women who are NOT doing jobs that they are more than capable of doing. No one stops to count how many of us there are who are still blocked from doing what we can do and who are kept from contributing to what our nation needs — blocked by some outrageous notion that women simply can't do this or that.

Why there are still folks — and I must be honest and say that they are men and some women too — who say with firm conviction that a woman's place is to stand behind her man. But as I was so fond of saying to Spelman College women, the problem with a woman standing behind her man is that she can't see where she's going!

Let me pose a question: Could it be that as we move into the next century, styles of leadership which are thought to be more associated with women than men may turn out to be more effective, as well as more humane, ways to lead? I hasten to say that I don't think leadership styles are carried on the chromosomes. Women, like men, learn to lead in a certain way.

How women and how men lead is to a large measure a reflection of how we are socialized. It seems to me that because of ongoing conditions in our society, we womenfolk learn to lead with a more inclusive style, a more decentralized manner than most men. If this is so, and I believe that it is, then we must ask: Is the inclusive and cooperative style of leadership that is associated with women not only a more pleasant way, but ultimately a more effective way to carry out tasks than the "every man for himself and against all others" form of extreme competition that is often, though not always, associated with men?

So how do we strike out on a new course on the question of leadership? I think we do so by being terribly honest about who our current leaders are, and creative about who might be our leaders in the next century. We examine the traditional models of success and entertain the possibility that some other values and people might also serve us well.

I am absolutely convinced that one of those values that we must champion, as women have done traditionally, is a value that is the ultimate expression of leadership. And that is service to others. After all, as Elie Wiesel, a victim of the Holocaust and one of our great humanitarians has put it, "Our lives do not belong to us alone. They belong to those who need us most." Or in the words of one of my heroes, Spelman College graduate and president of the Children's Defense Fund, Marian Wright Edelman, "Doing for others is just the rent you pay for living on this earth."

We womenfolks can – and must – take our rightful places in the coming millennium.

In my lifetime, I have been fortunate to experience the joys that come from engaging in meaningful service to my community. But over the past year, I have had an experience that is truly remarkable as I serve as a big sister in the Big Brothers/Big Sisters Program in Atlanta. My little sister is 12-year-old Maranda Smith. But I must tell you that she is a thief. Maranda has stolen my heart, and she refuses to give it back.

Serving as Maranda's mentor is also one of the most direct ways in which I can participate in the process of "growing" one of tomorrow's leaders. The hours I spend with Maranda every week are good for her and contribute to her development. But when I am helping Maranda with her homework, when we are having "girl talk," when I give her lots of hugs, and when I help her to dream about and prepare for going to college — it all brings so much joy to me.

As we womenfolk prepare to become the leaders of the next millennium, our image of leadership will not be about bossing people around but consulting with them about where it is you can go collectively. Our notion of leadership focuses on how you can serve others rather than how you can be served. And I hope that when you close your eyes and imagine yourself as a leader in whatever profession or circumstance you desire, you see yourself above all else, expressing qualities of honesty, integrity, compassion and persistent, hard work. For these are the qualities that have characterized all true leaders of all time.

We womenfolks can and must take our rightful places in the coming millennium. And of course, that means that we must claim the fact that we belong in the House and in the Senate too! And one day, one of us will be "the one" in a big house, a White House.

And so, into this new century each of us has the responsibility to work toward that day when we womenfolks, and that means all of us womenfolks in all of our diversity, will finally have full economic, political and social equality.

I am so proud to be an alumna of a college, Mills College, where women, and some righteous men, too, are deeply involved in the struggle for that new day in a new millennium. To arrive at that new day in a new millennium — will it be easy? Of course not! But we really have no choice but to engage in the struggle for that victory.

Chris Coleman

Chris Coleman is a technology marketer who has launched, branded and promoted tech products for more than 200 companies worldwide. She founded Folio Z, the first technology advertising agency in the Southeast.

Coleman is a member of the Technology Executives Roundtable and the National Speakers Association. She was honored this year by *Atlanta Magazine* as a "Woman Making a Mark," and by Women in Technology International as a "Woman Forging the Future." She was instrumental in the creation of the Technology Association of Georgia, which is the largest organization of its kind in the United States.

Coleman is the author of *The Green Banana Papers: Marketing Secrets for Technology Entrepreneurs*.

WHAT DO MEN KNOW ABOUT TECHNOLOGY THAT WOMEN DON'T?
Chris Coleman to the WebGRRLS/eBusiness Expo

Minneapolis, Minnesota — May, 2001

What do men know about technology that women don't? In a word: nothing.

Despite that, only four of the 200-plus technology companies I've worked with over the years have been run by female CEOs.

Why?

Is it because so many women have convinced themselves that technology is still a "guy's job?"

For the past 17 years, I've had lots of opportunities to see how we women interview for our dream jobs, how we do the work once we're hired, and how we interpret signals along the way. And I'm convinced that we often sabotage ourselves without ever knowing it.

There's nobody to blame here: not our male colleagues, not ourselves. If we're serious about balancing the gender gap in the tech sector, we need to get over the idea that we have to master the game before we get a chance to play.

My first tech job was at a software company, where I was hired for my writing ability, not my technical acumen. I was in over my head, and I hated it. For more than six months, I told co-workers (and anybody else who would listen) that since I didn't understand the business yet, they could expect lots of mistakes.

Looking back, this was both a sympathy ploy ("Give me a break, I'm the new girl!") and a preemptive move against anybody who wondered why in the world I'd been chosen for this job. By my standards, not knowing enough meant I'd already failed.

Since then I've interviewed hundreds of people for my own business, and I realize how pointless my anxiety was. Nobody cared what I didn't know. I was being paid for what I did know. It was my job to learn the rest by asking questions and paying attention.

Last year I interviewed two Web developers with similar resumes.

Both were very desirable candidates. Candidate No. 1, a female, told me, "I'm very good at _____, but I still don't have much experience in _____." Candidate No. 2, a male, said, "I just finished a terrific site for Procter & Gamble. Here's the URL if you'd like to take a look."

Turns out the woman had produced nearly three dozen sites, two of which are the top-drawing URLs in their categories. The man's work for Procter & Gamble, done during an internship, was his only real-world experience. So why did Candidate No. 1 present herself as a glass half empty?

Maybe she thinks she must master her craft before she's entitled to be paid for it. If so, she's mistaken. Working in IT isn't like practicing medicine without a license. The smartest, most accomplished people in this business learned 98 percent — or more — of what they know on the job. The secret is to focus on what you do know — not what you don't.

There are four more traps that can derail a technology career, and women seem to fall into them more frequently than men. Forewarned is forearmed, so here goes:

Trap #1: The shrinking violet. If you're an outsider who wants to move into the tech sector, you can't do it on tiptoe. Bold steps are the only ones that work. Network, network, network! Go to meetings where you don't know the people and don't understand the jargon. Guess what? Nobody knows what all those acronyms mean. Not even the old-timers.

Trap #2: Let the work speak for itself. It won't, speak for itself, that is. Once you're inside the walls of a technology company (or any company for that matter), you have to be as good at developing ideas and relationships as you are at producing good work. This doesn't mean all tech companies are rife with politics — some are, some aren't — but the business moves so fast that if you don't speak up, you won't be heard.

Trap #3: Don't move until you're positive you're right. Baloney! A sense of urgency is a must in this business. Caution has its place, but if you hate making decisions based on incomplete information, technology probably isn't for you. On the other hand, if every job you've ever had moves too slowly, you'll love it here.

Trap #4: Waiting for consensus. General agreement? Yes. Total agreement? No. Consensus doesn't exist in this business. As you move up the leadership ladder, you'll find that action counts. Women who understand how to build coalitions across departmental or company lines are the big winners.

Finally, fortune favors the daring. If you're a woman peering through the fence at a technology career, look around for the gate. I guarantee it's there. Your job is simply to swing it open and stride on in. Believe me: You'll figure out the rest as you go along.

Betty Ann Cook

Dr. Betty Ann Cook was appointed to the Georgia Board of Pardons and Paroles in 1997.

Cook has served on many boards, including Research Atlanta, TEAM Georgia and Georgians for Children. She is a founding member of the Governor's Commission on Family Violence and the Georgia Network of Children's Advocacy Centers Advocates Council. In 2000, she received the Women Looking Ahead Award in Government.

In 1999, Cook founded "Girl Talk, Heart to Heart," a volunteer intervention program for female juvenile offenders designed to curb youth violence and reduce the number of repeat female offenders. The six-week program enhances girls' decision-making skills and helps them establish relationships with positive-thinking women.

Cook is married and has one daughter, Candice Sherrie.

BRIDGING THE GAP IN THE CRIMINAL JUSTICE SYSTEM
Betty Ann Cook to the congregation of the Allen Temple AME Church (Excerpts)

Woodstock, Georgia — January, 2001

Today we pay tribute to the life and legacy of the Reverend Dr. Martin Luther King Jr. as we examine the theme, *Bridging the Gap.*

Just as Dr. King in his time became a drum major for equal justice and equal rights, today, we must pick up the torch in urban and rural Georgia, and lead our young people away from the darkness of drugs, alcohol, teen pregnancy and violence. We must deliver to our youth a message of hope that will propel their energies towards building a better world for all people, black and white.

We cannot let any issue stop us from continuing the journey towards economic and social justice that Dr. King, the late Rev. Hosea Williams, Rep. Grace Hamilton, Mrs. Coretta Scott King, Mayor Patsy Hilliard, Monica Kaufman, the Honorable Andrew Young, Sen. Charles Walker, Reps. Tyrone Brooks, Calvin Smyre, Kathy Ashe, Carl Epps, Maretta Taylor and others who have worked so hard to make a better world possible for African Americans.

Therefore, we must give credit to those men and women of courage for speaking out when those of lesser courage kept silent. Men like Atlanta's previous mayor, Ivan Allen; Police Chief Herbert T. Jenkins, who later served on the Kerner Civil Rights Commission; Sen. Zell Miller, who early in his first term addressed the flag issue; and Governor Roy Barnes, who is fighting for the well-being for all Georgia children.

We must never forget Ralph McGill, who through his newspaper put words and a face on the movement to feed the hungry, clothe the poor and house the homeless. Ralph McGill's columns taught us that justice should never be decided by the color of a person's skin or the size of their bank account.

If Dr. King were alive today, I'm sure that he would enjoy the progress we have made in bridging the gap between the races. However, I think he would be saddened and outraged by the disparate numbers of African Americans institutionalized in our jails and prisons.

Let's look at this more closely. In Georgia, African Americans represent approximately 28 percent of the entire population. However, we represent nearly 70 percent of the prison population in Georgia. You might say, maybe they committed the crimes.

State Rep. David Lucas, chair of the State Property and Institutions Committee of the House, read a research study from the parole board on the probability of going to prison in Georgia. He was shocked at its findings.

New research shows that spending more time in prison actually increases the likelihood of committing crime in the future.

What is the likelihood of going to a Georgia prison in your lifetime? According to the study, a Georgian has a one in 10 chance of going to prison in his or her lifetime. The findings of the study further concluded that a Georgian is twice as likely to go to prison as all U.S. citizens (10 percent v. 5 percent). Males in Georgia are twice as likely (18 percent) to go to prison than the average U.S. male (9 percent). Black males in Georgia stand a 38 percent chance of going to prison, as compared with 28 percent of black males nationwide; and lastly, females are more than twice as likely (2.5 percent) to wind up in a Georgia prison than they are nationwide (1.1 percent).

The report to the Georgia Parole Board further stated that Georgia's focus on prison construction, coupled with the lack of alternatives to incarceration for judges, has contributed to the greater probability of going to prison in our state.

Please hear this: There are people in our prisons today who should stay there and never leave. However, for nonviolent offenders, we need a greater range of alternatives before prison.

After studying the findings, Rep. Lucas asked Applied Research, an independent research group, to further examine incarceration patterns between urban and rural communities and between white and blacks. These findings yield the following. During the past five years, 37,000 nonviolent offenders have been sentenced to prison who matched the profiles of probationers sent to detention centers. Placement of just 5,500 of these individuals (one year's worth) would have saved the state over $56 million.

Additional findings from the study on the urban and rural arrest and incarceration rates showed the following. In Georgia, while the overall arrest and crime rates have declined, statewide incarceration rates have actually increased by 45 percent. The arrest rate for blacks is three times that of whites; in rural Georgia, there are 12 blacks sent to prison for drug offenses for every white, while in urban areas the ratio is nine blacks to one white. In 2000, out of a total of 4,100 entering the prison system for cocaine offenses, fully 83 percent were black and only 17 percent were white.

New research shows that spending more time in prison actually increases the likelihood of committing crime in the future. For example, a person who is sent to prison for stealing hub caps, goes to prison and learns how to steal a whole car! Can you see the problem? How can we bridge that gap?

We need to establish a new vision for community corrections, for if we keep doing what we're doing, we'll keep getting what we're getting. Statewide, 40 percent of all ex-offenders return to prison and approximately 60 percent of African Americans do the same.

We now are experiencing a brief moment of grace, a moment that will not last long, a moment that is upon Georgia policymakers and elected officials to bring equity and meaningful and productive change to the criminal justice system. Falling crime rates and a booming economy have ushered in this fleeting moment.

This is a chance for us, black and white, to come together and keep the dream of equal justice alive in our hearts.

It is true we must adopt aggressive programs that have a demonstrated track record of producing productive citizens. Education reform, adequate health care, support for working moms, attention to domestic violence and effective public safety support can all increase the community's well-being in the long run.

However, giving judges alternatives for nonviolent offenders is also an answer. It is effective, it works. Judges want it and, believe it or not, it saves tax payers money. More importantly, it saves lives.

Giving judges alternatives to incarceration for nonviolent offenders — alternatives to include adequate substance abuse and mental health treatment or other help that offenders need to succeed in life and remain crime-free — is a viable alternative and partial solution to the inequities in arrests, sentencing and punishment in Georgia.

Policymakers, ministers, educators, law enforcement officials and concerned leaders are looking at the inequities in sentencing and punishment as we speak. And this is not a Democratic or Republican issue, or a liberal or conservative issue, but one of right and responsibility.

This new vision for community corrections delivers what the public wants. It delivers safety through rational supervision policies, risk management and tracking of offenders. It includes effective alternatives where the punishment fits the crime.

Dr. King reminds me of another dreamer whose vision he shared as he ministered to us. Joseph was the son of Israel. Israel had many children, but because Joseph was born during Israel's old age, he loved Joseph more. He made Joseph a coat of many colors, and Joseph's brothers were very jealous. Joseph was a dreamer. Joseph dreamed that his brothers would bow down to him. Because of their jealousy towards him, Joseph's brothers sold him into slavery. Joseph later became a servant of an Egyptian. And the Lord was with him and his master realized this. Joseph became a great man and later saved his family's lives. His brothers did eventually bow down to him.

Today, we bow to this son of the South, a preacher man with a Ph.D., whose birth we celebrate for the first time this year as a national holiday in all 50 states. In 1963, he never thought his courageous work would be recognized by the Alfred Nobel Society, nor did he realize how far his dream would go. His dream lives on today through us.

So, let us go back into our communities and teach the teachings of Dr. King to our youth. We must take away the guns and dope and give our children and family our time, discipline, responsibility, a sense of fairness, books, love, values and hope.

In the parole system in Georgia, we decided some time ago that enough is enough. We decided that given all that we see everyday with adult offenders, we had to do something to get to kids in communities throughout the state. We initiated our Drug Violence Prevention and Education program. The staff of this program travel the state and discuss with young folks the ravages of drugs and violence in our communities. Last year alone, our staff made presentations to more than 30,000 school children, teachers and school administrators. In addition, I founded and participate in a program that we call "Girl Talk, Heart to Heart." This program allows me and female parole employees to meet with young female offenders in the custody of the Department of Juvenile Justice to discuss life and why it must be lived with character.

At the parole board, we are attempting to create opportunities for youth to learn new ways of thinking and behaving so that they can learn how to make better choices.

Many of the adults who come to us are abused, neglected, low achievers who are often pushed to the periphery of our schools and social systems. Their risk factors have accumulated and their opportunities have been limited.

Of course, these folks must be held accountable for the crimes that they have committed. However, punishment must be balanced with rehabilitation in an environment which fosters positive, pro-social and productive behavior.

This is the challenge Dr. King would want us to face as we engage in "Bridging the Gap" in the new millennium.

Cathy Cox

Cathy Cox serves as Georgia's Secretary of State; she is the first woman elected to the position in Georgia. She has worked to enhance customer service and strengthen protections for Georgia consumers and has been instrumental in Georgia's efforts to address the problem of antiquated and inaccurate voting equipment. Her bill will move the state to a modern uniform system of voting by July 2004.

Cox has received numerous honors for her public service, including being chosen as the 2000 Woman of the Year by the Georgia Commission on Women. Mercer School of Law awarded her the 1999 Distinguished Alumna Award and *Georgia Trend* magazine has chosen her as one of the 100 Most Influential Georgians for the past three years.

Cox and her husband, Mark Dehler, an attorney, reside in northeast Atlanta.

WOMEN AS ENTREPRENEURS

Cathy Cox to the Georgia Women's Entrepreneurs Conference GWEN (Excerpts)

Augusta, Georgia — April, 2001

I'm a great believer that much of what comes to us in life flows directly from the choices we make as individuals. When we celebrate women entrepreneurs, we cannot help but remember that each of you has made a choice in your life – a choice to take a big risk to achieve even greater rewards.

In fact, it's a good bet that there is not one woman in this room who hasn't had to overcome personal or professional hurdles to make her own way as a business owner.

The hurdle might have come from a banker or a potential customer who had doubts about your ability – who, maybe without knowing it, questioned whether you had what it takes to succeed, doubts that arose simply because of your gender. It might have been a course of study in college that you had to work and work and work to finally master. It might have been a difficult personal relationship or family tragedy that, if you had let it, could have undermined your confidence and discouraged you from your fulfilling your dreams of building your own enterprise.

For those of you with children, it might have been the tug of war in your own heart and mind as to whether your professional ambitions would somehow compromise your ability to be the parent you know your children need.

But you have made that choice – the choice to set your own course. You decided not to wait for others to show the way but are clearing a path of your own making.

A young woman went to visit a fortune-teller for a reading. After studying the woman's palm the old soothsayer gazed deeply into the crystal ball.

"Hmmm", she said, "What I see is not good. You will be poor and unhappy until you're 45 years old."

"Oh my goodness," the young woman asked, "What happens then?"

"Ah", said the fortune-teller, "Then, you'll get used to it!"

Many of you I'm sure have broken new ground – in your industry or in your community. And as Georgia's first female secretary of state, I know a little something about being first. When you are first, in politics just like in business, you're going to face some challenges, and you have to overcome a lot of traditions and stereotypes.

But what a great time to be a business owner in Georgia. As we enter a new century, Georgia is experiencing an historic wave of growth virtually unmatched anywhere in the nation. Our state's economy today is more than 51 percent bigger than it was just a decade ago and much more diverse. It is powered by a broad-based industrial sector, a rich consumer market, extensive technology infrastructure and unprecedented high-tech and construction job growth.

In the United States, women now own more than 9 million businesses. That's more than twice the number we had in 1990. Never has there been a better time for women-owned businesses, especially in Georgia. Today, Georgia ranks first in the growth of women-owned businesses. Think about that. Nowhere else in the nation is female entrepreneurship growing as fast. That's a tremendous achievement, and you made it happen. Yes, today Georgia ranks 10th in the nation in overall number of women-owned firms.

But it wasn't always that way. Just 38 years ago in April of 1963, Georgia Governor Carl Sanders gave a speech to a group of young women in which he said this about their career goals:

"I can think of no better way to demonstrate one's skills than to rear a family, keep house, belong to the PTA, grow a garden and give a husband and children the love, devotion and guidance they need to lead full, rich lives.

"What happens in the home overflows into the community and for that reason there is no better place to practice your knowledge and skills than right in your own living room and kitchen."

My point is not to make fun of Governor Sanders. He is my friend, and he was an outstanding and progressive governor whose leadership in the law and in civic affairs continues to this day. No, in 1963, he simply expressed the prevailing view of his time – accepted by nearly all, women and men alike. With the exception of a few fields like teaching and nursing, the proper place for a woman was in the home – and only in the home.

And those attitudes were the product of a long tradition. Just think about that great novel of southern challenge and triumph, that's been much in the news the last few weeks, *Gone With the Wind*. Absolutely nothing was more scandalous to Atlanta society than when Scarlett took over and ran – and ran very successfully – her husband's business after he was killed defending her honor. A woman running a business, hiring and firing, making money – now that was quite a scandal!

> *Today, Georgia ranks first in the growth of women-owned businesses. Think about that. Nowhere else in the nation is female entrepreneurship growing as fast.*

How far we have come here in Georgia. How much brighter are the opportunities for all our citizens, black and white, women and men, to fulfill their own dreams of business success.

Last year there were more than 240,000 women-owned businesses in our state, accounting for more than 37 percent of all the state's businesses. That's right, nearly four in 10 businesses in Georgia are now owned by women. Those women-owned enterprises employ more than 1.1 million people and generate more than $182 billion, yes ... BILLION ... dollars in economic activity. I am absolutely certain that those trends will continue, and in fact are likely to accelerate in the years ahead.

If you look back to the end of World War I, you see a very different Georgia. No woman in Georgia, white or black, rich or poor, was permitted to vote in any election. Not surprisingly, with no voice in the choosing of our leaders, the laws of the land were heavily stacked against women. Women lacked equal property rights, had few opportunities for advanced education, were barred from many professions and bore the heavy burden of taxation without representation.

And Georgia has the dubious distinction of, in 1919, becoming the first state in the nation to reject the 19th amendment to the U.S. Constitution, which extended the right to vote to American women. Not until 1920, when a sufficient number of other states ratified the suffrage amendment, did women cast their first votes in Georgia elections.

Today, not only is the chief elections official of this state a woman, but the director of our state elections division is also a woman. That's quite a change. In the Georgia of today, female voters now make up a healthy majority of the electorate and women have comprised about 54 percent of the total vote in every recent election.

And not only are women at the forefront in selecting our leaders, but more and more of us are earning election to higher office as well. Yes, I am the first female secretary of state, but consider also a woman as state school superintendent, women on both the Supreme Court and Court of Appeals, and women in growing numbers making their voices heard in the Georgia General Assembly.

In fact, the 2001 Legislative Session concluded just a few weeks ago with 37 women serving in the House of Representatives and 10 women in the State Senate. That translates into 20 percent of legislative offices in Georgia being held by women.

Yet even with all the progress women have made, on average, women still earn only 77 cents for each dollar earned by men doing the same job.

But I know this: The people in this room pay employees what they are worth, whether they are men or women. And so a wonderful benefit of this huge growth in female entrepreneurship is the assurance that we will take the final strides to wipe away the last remnants of pay inequity — because it's stupid, it's wrong and women business owners and CEOs are simply not going to let it continue.

As you continue to follow your dreams, building great businesses into even greater ones, I hope you will also take the time to open doors for a new generation of young women through mentoring programs. They need your intellect and your energy. And you'll be putting those meaningful words, "power through knowledge and wisdom through sharing" into action in a way that may transform a life, or even more than one.

It is an odd place to find inspiration, but in closing I'd like to leave you with a quote I came across recently in *U.S. News and World Report:*

"After years of analyzing what makes leaders most effective and figuring out who's got the right stuff, management gurus now know how to boost the odds of getting a great executive: *hire a female.*"

What took them so long to figure that out?

Emma J. Darnell

Emma Darnell is the vice chair of the Fulton County Board of Commissioners, District 5. She was chosen in a special election in 1992 and has been re-elected twice since that time. Commissioner Darnell is president of E.I. Darnell and Associates P.C.

As a commissioner, Darnell has focused on the delivery of improved services for minorities, women, senior adults and the poor. She is a member of the Judicial Council of the Christian Methodist Episcopal Church and serves as the chair of the board of trustees for West Mitchell Street CME Church. She is also a graduate of Leadership Atlanta and has received more than 200 awards for outstanding service to the Atlanta and Fulton County community, including the Doctor of Divinity degree, Honors Causa, Phillips (CME) School of Theology, International Theological Center in Atlanta in May of 2000.

TEACH THE WORDS

Emma I. Darnell to the National CME Annual Convocation
Birmingham, Alabama — September, 1995

> *"Teach the words to your children,
> and see that they do not forget them."*
> — Margaret Walker

It is interesting that during periods of progress and accomplishment, people often focus upon their past. After entering Canaan, Moses instructed the people about words — not strategies, but *words* that should remain in their hearts, not their PC's.

Two-thousand years later, in her poem, *Teach the Words*, Margaret Walker, borrowing from Moses, suggests that the same conduct may be relevant for our times. "Teach the words ... see that they do not forget them."

What words? And why do we need them now?

We have information. Information is everywhere. We have smart tags, pocket computers, remote car keys, faxes, PC's and the Palm. In the wireless age, we have so much information that we stay in a state of what one writer has called "perpetual distraction." And we are missing things. Important things.

"I wish I had listened," Isaiah Schoelts' father said when they told him his son had been shot at Columbine High School. "My boy told me he was having trouble at that school. I wish I had listened."

Why didn't he listen? Why couldn't he hear or see the evil that was around him? He was a good father, a good citizen who wanted only the best for his family. He had moved to the Denver suburbs primarily to ensure that his children would have "a better life." And now his son is dead, killed, according to the gunman, because "he was black."

Mr. Schoelts did not listen because he was mean or insensitive; most people are not. He listened, but he could not hear. He is not the only one.

Often, we do not hear. We do not hear the public housing resident who is unable to return to the "new" development because she could not

> *We have information.*
> *Information is everywhere.*
> *We have smart tags, pocket computers,*
> *remote car keys, faxes, PC's and the Palm.*
> *In the wireless age, we have so much*
> *information that we stay*
> *in a state of what one writer has called*
> *"perpetual distraction."*
> *And we are missing things.*
> *Important things.*

pass the housekeeping test. We do not hear the high school graduate who cannot read or write; the senior citizen who has been on a waiting list for "Meals on Wheels" for more that a year. We listen but cannot hear. With all of the information we receive, some things must be "tuned out."

However, it is different with the words. The words are in our hearts. The words tell stories — the stories of Frederick Douglas, Gabriel Prosser and Denmark Veasy, Harriett Tubman, Sojourner Truth and Rosa Parks.

The words tell the story of Montgomery, Birmingham and Memphis — stories that are invested with a people's pilgrimage and determination.

Words of explanation, words that explain not only who we are, but what we are, what we believe in and what we stand for. Words pertaining to our faith, moral lessons to be learned and followed.

Prophecies fail, tongues cease, even knowledge vanishes away. But love never fails. I have been young and now am old, yet have I not seen the righteous forsaken, or their seed begging bread. Words.

Dr. Martin Luther King Jr. once said, "There is nothing in all the world like freedom. It is worth living for. It is worth dying for. I would rather live in abject poverty and be free, than to have inordinate riches and lose my self-respect."

Teach the words!

Stacey H. Davis

Stacey H. Davis is president and chief executive officer of the Fannie Mae Foundation. The foundation is the largest in the country devoted to affordable housing issues, such as creating affordable homeownership and housing opportunities and building healthy neighborhoods.

Davis led Fannie Mae's Trillion Dollar Commitment initiative, a pledge to help 10 million families buy homes of their own by the year 2000.

Davis serves on the board of directors of the Policy Advisory Board of the Joint Center for Housing Studies at Harvard University, the Museum of African Art, the Washington Ballet, N Street Village, Social Compact and the Welfare to Work Partnership. She has also served as treasurer and chair of the Finance Committee for the Fulton-DeKalb Hospital Authority and on several other boards, including the Atlanta Urban League, Research Atlanta and the Herndon Foundation.

TAKE CARE OF THE TULIPS

*Stacey Davis to Trinity College,
Commencement Address (Excerpts)*
Washington, D.C. — May, 2001

I was thinking about what I might say to you today, what wisdom I might pass on. And I kept coming back to my nursery school teacher in Atlanta, Mrs. Annie Lou Hendricks. She is 97-years-old, and she traveled to be with us here today. She taught my father, my sister and me. Her school wasn't an imposing building; it was her house. What I remember most was the way she taught us about life. She did this in many different ways, and one of them was by teaching us how to plant tulips. Now, to a 4-year-old, it seemed magic. You plant them. You water them. You are patient, and you make sure nobody else tramples them. When spring comes, they bloom. "You've got to take care of the tulips," Mrs. Hendricks would say.

"Take care of the tulips" — in my time as an investment banker and as president of a foundation, I haven't come across better advice than that. And it's true that I'm only a few years further along in my journey than you are in all of yours. On this spring day, I wish I could tell you that your striving is over — and that this degree will guarantee you an easy and carefree life. But I can't.

Your struggles have been hard, but they are just beginning. I promise you, great opportunities are before you, but they bring with them new challenges. Of all the things I have learned, the lesson that most surprised me was that the higher you rise, the thinner the air — the more chauvinism, resistance, the more obstacles you will face.

Thank God, today women are in every profession, earning every kind of degree, doing every kind of work. There are women of color in each of these fields, too. But our less-enlightened past is not ancient history. We may be used to seeing women at work, but it's still a surprise to see women in authority, let alone in power.

Let me tell you what I mean. I am now the president of a foundation with over 100 employees that spends $110 million in grants and other activities each year.

Last year, I was visiting Los Angeles. At a social gathering, a man was pointed out to me across the room, who was the head of a nonprofit organization that was seeking money from our foundation. We'd never met personally, but he'd been sending me many e-mails. A friend brought me over and introduced me as "Stacey Davis, president of the Fannie Mae Foundation." He glanced quickly at me, and said to my friend, "She's not the president of the Fannie Mae Foundation. I know who the president of the Fannie Mae Foundation is." Now, obviously, he had a mental image of what the president of our foundation should look like — and I wasn't it. (Maybe it was the height that threw him off.)

Or the question I often get: "So, you're the head of the Fannie Mae Foundation?" Followed by: "Umm ... so who really runs the foundation?"

I have nothing to complain about. I have the chance to go to work every day, to do something I love, knowing that I am able to help a lot of people I will never meet while I do it. But I don't think I'm revealing any secret when I say that if you are a woman, and even more so a woman of color, you need to do more. You need to go above and beyond. You need to be better.

So how do you find the will to climb the next hill and the one after that? Well, I've already given you one suggestion: Remember to take care of the tulips. But there is a bit more to it than that. I have three answers, three things that have helped me enormously in my life. And with your permission I will share them.

The first answer is family. You are not walking alone. Going forward, perhaps your family and your friends won't have to make the financial sacrifices they made to get you through college, but you will need them even more. I have found that even when my family members are gone, I still rely on their spirit for support. And I can't tell you how many times, sitting through a boring meeting, I have brought my thoughts into balance by thinking of those I love. Parents and husbands and lovers and friends, I'm putting you on notice: You are still needed. Even if you're not asked, you're still needed.

The second answer is faith. There is tremendous strength in surrendering to belief. My own relationship with God has been a source of serenity, sanity and balance, no matter how crazy the situation. I have noticed that the older I get, a daily prayer has become more important to me, not less. Whenever you are tired, remember that Philippians says, "You can do all things through faith, that strengthens you."

And the third answer: You have not been brought this far, through all of your struggles, just for material gain. Remember that your true purpose in life is service. Gandhi once said, "You will only find yourself by losing yourself in service to others." I have had many wonderful professional experiences. But I can tell you that nothing compares to the joy of working at a foundation where I know that every ounce of energy is going toward helping others. I know that we are helping women who have never had a checking account, never had credit and never believed it would be possible to buy a home. More than just providing a safe place to live, we are giving women and families a chance to build wealth.

Remember what matters. You will go on; you will achieve great things; you will rise in your professions. You'll go on great vacations, but then you're back at your desk. You're going to buy a fine car, but some parking lot valet guy is going to wreck it. You will buy a fine bottle of wine, but you'll drink it all and it will be gone. But what will remain, will be your family, your faith and your commitment to serve others. Those things last.

Today, you bid farewell to the women with whom you have gone to school. You will take different paths, and you may scatter to many corners of the country and possibly the world. Today, and tonight, celebrate. But know that tomorrow, your journey begins again. It won't be easy. Let me leave you with this thought from Scripture: "Be on your guard: Stand firm in your faith; be women of courage; be strong. Do everything in love."

And don't forget — take care of the tulips.

Stephanie Davis

Stephanie Davis is the first director of the Atlanta Women's Foundation, the only public foundation in Atlanta committed to making grants to projects that are changing the lives of women and girls. It is the fastest-growing women's fund in the country.

Davis is also the Rosalynn Carter honorary fellow in women and policy at Emory University. She serves on the board of directors of Women and Philanthropy and the National Health Law Program and is on the advisory board of the Women's Health Program of Blue Cross/Blue Shield. She is in the first group to be appointed to the City of Atlanta's Commission for Women.

Davis received the Women's Health and Well-being Advocacy Award from United Healthcare and the "Leading Lady" award from Seven Stages theater. She is a graduate of Leadership Atlanta.

ECONOMIC JUSTICE FOR WOMEN
Stephanie Davis to Women in Finance and Women in Media and Technology (Excerpts)
Atlanta — 2000 and 2001

What does economic justice for women mean? Think about the fact that women are still being paid 71 cents for every dollar earned by men, that sexual harassment is alive and well, that women are systematically kept from learning skills that would mean higher wages, and that our workplaces do not support the basic needs of a woman and her children.

Who needs economic justice? Refugee and immigrant women who are isolated in their communities, elderly women, women coming out of prison, women who have been left behind without the skills and resources necessary to support themselves and their children.

A woman in poverty is usually a woman *and child* in poverty. The cycle of poverty is vicious and complicated. The United States continually emphasizes the value of work and the importance of decreasing welfare roles. Yet few acknowledge the somber reality that most welfare recipients' new jobs pay far below the poverty line. In Atlanta, as urban sprawl continues to dictate the area's growth, the wide disparity of wealth intensifies. Job opportunities flourish in the wealthier northern counties that are out of reach of public transportation. The southern, inner city and rural areas have far fewer jobs that pay adequate wages. Poor women live paycheck to paycheck with little opportunity to move ahead and few career-training opportunities. Very few low-paying jobs offer benefits. Women on welfare and the working poor who are able to obtain employment are still not able to pull themselves up, out of poverty. This is partly due to the fact that the actual value of minimum wage in 1997 was 18.1 percent less than in 1979.

Georgia's Temporary Assistance to Needy Families (TANF) is a state-run welfare program that provides four years of monthly cash assistance for poor families with children under 18. The overwhelming majority of TANF recipients are women and children. In 1996, Assistance to Families with Dependent Children (AFDC) was replaced by TANF, decreasing the income eligibility.

Confusing and elaborate TANF procedures discourage those who qualify for assistance from applying. The families who do apply can be penalized for not meeting required protocols, even though their ability to meet these requirements are seldom assessed. As a result, many families who do qualify for assistance today do not receive it. There is a vast discrepancy between the TANF requirements imposed on women and their ability to feed their families. This disconnect can lead to a pervasive feeling of being trapped by the system.

Since 1997, Georgia has seen a 53.8 percent decrease in the number of families receiving cash assistance. Most of these 61,994 families continue to live in poverty even when working. Nationwide, the average maximum monthly TANF allotment for a mother and two children in 1998 was $405 per month. Georgia's maximum award amount was $208 in 1998 and $280 in 2000.

Homelessness, the most dramatic result of poverty, also disproportionately affects women and children. Women and children are the fastest-growing population among homeless individuals. According to the Task Force for the Homeless, single women and women with children accounted for 69 percent of reported individuals requesting shelter in the Atlanta metropolitan area in 1999. A Ford Foundation study found that 50 percent of homeless women and children are fleeing abuse.

Affordable housing in the Atlanta metro area is a challenge. In Atlanta, the Fair Market Rent (FMR) as established by HUD for a one-bedroom unit is $590, and housing is considered affordable if it costs 30 percent of the renter's income or less. A minimum-wage worker earning $10,712 per year can afford to pay only $267.80 for monthly rent. In Atlanta, a three-person household receiving the maximum TANF assistance can afford $84 in rent.

According to the U.S. Department of Labor, the number of working women has doubled from 30 million in 1970, to 60 million in 1997. Women accounted for 46.6 percent of the Atlanta labor force in 1999, and it is estimated that women will represent 56 percent of the work force by 2006. In terms of male-to-female earnings, Georgia ranks 27th in the country, with women earning an average 71 cents to every male dollar. Since 1963 when the Equal Pay Act was signed, women have closed the wage gap at a rate of less than one penny per year. And if single working mothers earned as much as their male counterparts, their family incomes would increase by 17 percent and their poverty rates would be cut in half, from 25.3 to 12.6 percent.

We have also learned that economic justice makes good birth control. Give a girl the chance to fulfill her dream of owning her own business, and getting pregnant loses some of its appeal. Where would all of us be if someone, probably many people along the way, had not believed in us and provided us with access and resources? That is all poor women and girls want. Someone to believe in them and access to a better life with a job that pays a little more than it costs to keep their kids in child care, a little more so they don't have to go back to the man that used to beat them, a little more so they can hold their head up with self-respect.

The Atlanta Women's Foundation is a catalyst for change in the lives of women and girls. We know through our grant-making and our programs that progress towards social change and economic justice is hard to calibrate and it takes a great deal of patience to see tangible results. Action on these issues will take many forms and we urge concerned citizens to put their philanthropy — their thoughtful and consistent giving — where they think it can make a lasting and strategic difference.

Many of these issues suggest a change in policy, so we encourage people to search out those organizations that not only help individuals but are also working towards an equal and just society. It is also important to affect change by writing a letter to a policymaker or an editor, mentoring a girl or boy, volunteering where one's skills and talent will actually turn something around for somebody or for a whole group of people. It is in this way that we can *let every voice be heard*, so that all of us are respected and feel worthwhile, have chances and choices and equal voices, and know that we truly are our sister's keepers.

Sadie Jo Dennard

Sadie Jo Dennard is assistant region manager for Georgia Power's metro east region. She works with legislators and community leaders to foster economic expansion and community improvement initiatives throughout DeKalb and Rockdale counties.

Dennard is a member of the Atlanta Board of Education. During her tenure as president in 1999, the board launched the school's first charter school, piloted two year-round schools and implemented a comprehensive facility study. She received the Award for Distinguished Service from the National School Board Association in 2001.

Dennard serves on the Georgia School Board Association board of directors, as well as the boards of Public Broadcasting Atlanta/WPBA and the Georgia Partnership for Excellence in Education. She is a member of the Atlanta Business League and the Metro Coalition of 100 Black Women.

Dennard has one daughter, Brook.

WORK-FORCE PREPARATION
Sadie Jo Dennard to the faculty, students and parents at Atlanta Area Tech (Excerpts)
Atlanta — October, 1994

This is the age of new technologies and telecommunications. Competition is a way of life. It's not just for some; competition affects everyone. Change is the constant in this new world of information. Whether we're talking about jobs, business, industry or government, we're talking about constant change and the growth opportunities and challenges that change creates.

Today's successful organizations are structured for spontaneous alignment and quick responses to opportunities and challenges brought about through change. The successful work force operates with greater flexibility, behaviors and attitudes that are customer-focused and results-driven.

Significant changes in private industry, of the magnitude brought about by the need for information and knowledge, are almost always accompanied and sustained through the development and passage of strong public policy. Public policy is the way that we formalize new releases of energy into the marketplace.

Successful organizations drive the initiation of public policy to establish a firm launch pad from which to operate. There always exist a relationship between the innovators and the implementers.

There is an inherent need for public policy to create private initiatives. There is a duality in place between public policy and the initiatives that a man named Adam Smith talked about in a book he wrote, *Inquiry Into the Wealth of Nations*. Smith wrote about the need to deregulate government and the freeing of the energies of people to hustle in the marketplace, to identify demand and to create the supply to meet the demand.

In 1956, the faculty of Columbia University convinced President Eisenhower that one of the ways to stimulate the economy in America was to build an interstate highway system. At the time, our country needed an I-75, an I-85 and an I-95 that would run from Maine to

Florida and we needed a revised Route 66. Eisenhower used his influence, and the 82nd Congress enacted such legislation. Out of this came a new kind of construction energy that freed the marketplace.

In 1957, two young men in Memphis, Tenn., decided that if in fact a super highway system was to be built, and if the automotive industry building at that point about 5.1 million cars a year was to double, then more people would buy new cars, start traveling the highways, and they would need a place to sleep and eat along the way. So they became the nation's innkeepers. Everywhere the roads crossed, a Holiday Inn was built. And everywhere a Holiday Inn was built, Gulf Oil Company built a service station. Then somebody created a credit card, and more new energy was released into the market place.

> *I want to see us as a community really get focused on the critical need to fully prepare our young people to lead successful lives.*

The energy was initiated because public policy provided the basis for private initiative to borrow money, to spend money, to create jobs, to hire people — by design, with intentions, folks worked together to make it happen. The colleges and universities worked together to produce talented graduates with advanced technical degrees, and the vocational and technical high schools produced a very talented labor pool to innovate and implement. There was collaboration, common goals and relationships. A partnership was in place, a public/private partnership.

I want to see the same type of energy released today, and I want the product to be young men and women who, whenever they are ready, are prepared to contribute and participate in Georgia's economy. I want to see us as a community really get focused on the critical need to fully prepare our young people to lead successful lives. I want to be involved as a business person and a policymaker, working with educators, parents, legislators, business, government, industry and university representatives, thinking, planning and implementing the same way as the Holiday Inn boys. I want to see local public school systems operating like successful organizations — seeing an opportunity and filling the void. This can only occur through a public/private partnership.

Education and economics go together — they always have. Education is economic freedom. Education is the economic engine of the South and of the world. But where is the urgent flood of energy to really get our young people prepared to successfully contribute and participate in our economy? I will not believe nor accept that it is our strategy to import the employees that Georgia needs.

> *I will not believe nor accept that it is our strategy to import the employees that Georgia needs.*

In addition to teaching every child to read by third grade, become mathematically and technology literate in a safe school environment taught by highly qualified and caring teachers, schools must also expose students and teachers to the new job demands of our evolving economy. We must equip students with the skills needed to be successful entrepreneurs, employers or employees. Schools are the best environment in which to prepare students to lead productive lives. Schools are the best setting to prepare our youth to overcome the economic challenges they will face.

For many different reasons, all of our young people are not going directly from high school to a two- or four-year college or university. Some will choose to enter the work force. Some will need to continue to work. These young people need to be prepared to excel. They must know how to access and utilize knowledge, and have multiple skills and high flexibility. They will be called upon to conceptualize, to invent, to implement, to evaluate, to assess, to market, to distribute, to transmit, to generate and then start again. Students and teachers need opportunities to have exposure to real-world applications for science, mathematics

I believe that the democratization of our society may well rest in the hands of the classroom teacher who is the fulcrum around which most educational experiences revolve.

and technology. Parents need this exposure as well. We must be more aggressive in our efforts to establish apprenticeships and internships with business and industry for our students.

There are no short cuts to being well prepared. Whether parents help their children choose to continue their education through the military, at a technical school or a liberal arts college, they will need to know, understand and possess the skills that business, industry, colleges and the military expect and value.

My community, we must get busy. Our young people are dropping out of school and into our prison system at staggering rates. AIDS is infecting our next generation of fathers and mothers.

The human, ethical and moral reasons for equality of opportunity have existed for nearly 2,000 years. And I believe that the democratization of our society may well rest in the hands of the classroom teacher who is the fulcrum around which most educational experiences revolve. Kahlil Gibran, when asked to speak to the people on the teacher, said that the teacher shares not his knowledge but his wisdom, leading the learner to the threshold of his own mind.

Our young people deserve to be taught the value of freedom and responsibility. A highly skilled, productive human being contributes little to a democratic society unless he is cognizant of his responsibilities to himself as a human being, for his value judgments, for his conduct as an individual and as a social being.

We already know all we need to know to make a difference. What's missing is true commitment to our children's future. The commitment cannot be accomplished over the Internet. The size of the commitment that is required is hands-on. It means each of us has to get involved. We have to share our knowledge, time and energy. We must share a commitment to fuel a new energy into the market: young men and women prepared to participate in the economic growth of our communities.

Nellie Dunaway Duke

Nellie Dunaway Duke is the chair of the Georgia Commission on Women, an organization dedicated to advancing the health, educational, economic, social and legal status of women in Georgia. She is also CEO of the Georgia Woman of the Year Committee Inc.

Duke has served on numerous boards, including Possible Woman Enterprises, the Older Women's League, Georgia State University's Women's Resource Center and the Atlanta Women's Network. She is a founder of the Carroll Association for Prevention of Sexual Assault, the West Georgia Women's Forum, the Georgia Women's Alliance and Stopping Violence Where We Live.

In 2001, Duke received the Leadership Award from Women in Technology International and was named to the 100 Most Powerful Women List by *Women Looking Ahead*.

Duke is married to W. Henry Duke; they have five children and 10 grandchildren.

CHARACTERISTICS WHICH LEAD TO SUCCESS
Nellie Duke to the "Wise Women Speak" Conference
Atlanta — May 2001

It brings me great joy to be able to address this beautiful group of mothers and daughters. It does make me a bit fearful that I am billed under the title, "Wise Women Speak." It is my contention that those who think that they are wise, just may not be! In any case, I take the opportunity with joy. I have served on the Georgia Commission on Women since it was created in 1992. I have served as chair since 1994, and am proud that I have been able to join with others to make a difference in Georgia, and the United States, for women and girls. I didn't wake up one day and find that I was considered wise! I am 70-years-old, and my knowledge or wisdom has been accumulating throughout my lifetime.

I grew up in a little mill village in northwest Georgia, in a very sheltered environment. Both of my parents worked in the mill, my father as a steamfitter and my mother as a textile worker. My mother was a very special influence on my life. I think I got my activist mentality from her, although she had little outlet for hers. She and my dad were involved in organizing labor unions in the 1930's. My mother was so good at it, they made her a supervisor. Looking back, I believe they did that to get her out of the union! Even though she worked full-time, she found time to get to all my school activities, helped with parties and was always available whenever I got into trouble. The school I attended until 10th grade belonged to the company. They sponsored recreation and had a "company store" where you could buy on credit until payday. They even sponsored a minor league baseball team, built a huge swimming pool and held summer activities for the children of working mothers. During WWII, I held my first job, taking care of smaller children in the company daycare center. I know now that the company was progressive in many ways.

There was one way I was deprived. I never saw or met anyone who was not like me! There was no diversity in our little village, and even at Girl's High School, the school was racially segregated. And no boys were there either. We very quickly learned that if you took geometry, physics or chemistry, then you got to go two blocks down the street to Boy's High. If you played basketball, games were at Boy's High, cheerleaders attended football games and half the cheerleaders were boys. So, what did I do? I took chemistry and geometry, though they were considered subjects for boys at that time, and I played basketball and ran for cheerleader, and won. I was in my thirties before I had friends of color, or of any culture and socio-economic level other than my own. Yes, I was deprived. I graduated from high school when I was barely 16, and I married when I was still 18. I had attended "business school" and worked in advertising and sales for J.C. Penney while playing semi-pro basketball.

After marriage, I didn't work until my five children were all in school, but I did do community service as a volunteer in schools, PTA, church and the recreation league where I coached basketball. When we moved to Carrollton, I became education and youth director at our church, then Teen Club director for the city recreation department. In 1970, I went to work for the American Cancer Society in education and fund-raising. After 12 years, I retired because of my health, but I never stopped being an advocate for the rights of women and children.

> *I was in my thirties before I had friends of color, or of any culture and socio-economic level other than my own. Yes, I was deprived.*

I think it was in 1976 when I realized that women were second-class citizens. I read a footnote in a law book that said, "The above does not apply to women, idiots or children." I became West Georgia's area coordinator for ERA Georgia, and the rest is history. There are no such footnotes in Georgia's laws today, and I know that I have played a small role in bringing about that change. I have served on numerous boards, committees and authorities, but none has been so satisfying as what I am doing now.

The mission of the Commission on Women is to advance the health, educational, economic, social and legal status of the women of Georgia.

To accomplish that, we held public hearings to establish priorities. They are health, violence, discrimination, sexual harassment and child care/child support issues. We also try to provide recognition for the accomplishments of Georgia women, especially through Georgia Woman of the Year, Women in Sports Day and Women's History Month. We support legislation that will help women and families and oppose that which we consider harmful.

There are a few characteristics that jump out at me when I think of what I should suggest to you to help attain success and power, if you think of success as power. First, identify your call or your goals. Then, establish a commitment. Sometimes, it takes courage. To gain credibility, honesty and integrity are essential. You must communicate widely, and you always need to show compassion and understanding of others, their selves, their status and their ideas. Those are the six C's. Now for the seventh, and one of the most important Cs ... collaboration! Nobody ever accomplished much of anything without the help of others. Your life's work will be easier if you do. And be sure that credit is given to others, credit for their ideas, their support, their accomplishments.

Let's review: Accept the call, or mission; establish a commitment; exhibit courage; be credible; always communicate the message; show compassion to others; collaborate to maximize your own potential; and give credit to others!

Gail Evans

Gail Evans was executive vice president of Domestic Networks for the CNN News Group, in charge of program and talent development. She is a member of the CNN Executive Committee and is past chairperson of the CNN programming task force.

Evans is a member of the President's Commission on White House Fellows and the Committee 200, The International Women's Forum. She serves on the board of trustees at Kennesaw State University and the board of visitors at the Georgia State University School of Law. She also has been a member of the Citizens Review Panel of the Juvenile Court of Atlanta.

Evans has served as chairperson of the Georgia Endowment for the Humanities and as a trustee of the Radio and Television News Directors Foundation. She is a graduate of Leadership Atlanta.

BEING THERE

Gail Evans to the Atlanta Women's Foundation (Excerpts)

Atlanta — September, 2000

The way women will make it to the top and be really successful is to look to each other for support. You know what that's all about. It's about us being smarter. It's about us caring for each other and not letting anybody divide us. It's about being there. It really is about being there for each other.

But it's also about teaching each other. Over the years, I have frequently gone to meetings where there were only a few women in the room. You don't go to a meeting without speaking. When it's your turn, you don't pass if you're there with the big boss. One day I said, "No matter how much Ted (Turner) intimidates me by his brilliance and by his visionary thinking, (I'm clear on how much smarter he is than I am) I am going to make sure that I have something to say when I'm in the meeting." And for years, I used to rehearse the night before what I was going to say.

Part of how you get known and part of how you play smarter is to make sure people know that you exist.

Looking at this room is great: There are no empty seats in the front row. Women come into a meeting, and they head for the back row or they head for the middle or they head for their friend. But the action is in the front. The boss notices the person he or she is making eye contact with. If you're going to get ahead, you have to be smart and you have to know where you are. You are who you say you are. You can invent and reinvent yourself.

One of the things I feel really strongly about is that women have to support each other in our successes, not in our failures. I think one of the things that has happened to us over the years is that we have been great at being with each other when it didn't work out. When you didn't get what you wanted, when you didn't get the promotion, all of your girlfriends were there with the greatest support. We need to change, ladies. We need to be there with the greatest support, whether we love her or don't love her, when she gets the promotion — because the person who got the promotion knows something that you don't know. There's a reason why they got that promotion. And part of what you have to learn is that there is something to be learned there.

There's something about asking the questions. You need to know what the other people in your company earn. You need to know what the perks are. Now, it may seem our mothers and fathers brought us up to say that's dirty stuff that we don't want to talk about, but how are you going to know? It's not published, except for the chairman. It's not in the newspaper. So you need to be willing to try to find out, because that's how you're going to know what you deserve and what you can have.

Here is something else that you have to think about. Two people get promotions on the same day to the same level. There's one really good office, and there's one sort of mediocre office. You're a nice girl, and he's not so nice. He's clear which office he wants. You're pretty clear, too. But how are you going to fight over an office? It's ridiculous. So you do what we all learned. You say, "I'm not going to be a jerk; he can have the office." And you take the other office. A year later, why does everybody think he's more important than you are? Well, because to everybody else, the office counts. Find a nice way to do it, but don't give it up.

If we want to change the way it is at the office, if we want to change the world, we have to have power. That's part of why, when you look at the Atlanta Women's Foundation, it's about helping women to have the tools and the power to move ahead in their lives and their careers. We have to amass the power or we can't change things.

One of the great trends of today is that women are leaving corporate America to found their own small businesses. That's wonderful on one level, but I also am a little frightened by it because the Fortune 1000 control how we live, how we act and a lot of how we think. If we start leaving because we don't like the way the big corporation behaves, we're not going to be able to be there and change it. And while I love all of the books that are out there that propose the theories of the feminization of the workplace, it hasn't happened yet. I think that the progress we've made is great on some levels, but on the higher levels, it is, at best, creeping incrementalism. It hasn't happened yet. And we need to be there. We need to be there as women. We need to be there in all of our diverse ways, to make sure that the companies that lead our lives do it responsibly. We're all equal workers out there, but what the women bring to the table is a little different.

Somebody here today was telling me about how at her company they explained to her that the role of women was to be collegial. And she said she wanted to be aggressive. The men kept explaining to her that she was there because it was supposed to be collegial and she was supposed to help with the relationship part, to make everything work. But she wanted to be an aggressive salesperson. In fact, I've banned the word *assertive*. I think assertive is a word that somebody dreamed up so we would think we weren't supposed to be aggressive. If aggressive is a good word about a salesman, it's a good word about a saleswoman. Let's park *assertive*.

There's another word I want to part with, too, and that's *hope*. Everybody loves the word, hope. It's a really nice, feminine word. And we love it, but you know what? There's not much action in hope. "I hope I'm going to get the promotion" doesn't cut it. You have to learn to make a request to see what's possible. And that's really, really tough for a lot of us.

This is about business. This is, to a lot of people, about getting ahead and getting power. And if you give it away, somebody's always going to be there to take it. You need to be willing to take the risk to be *stupid*. I always love that. I think one of the great things for women is that we are actually willing to be stupid. We could say something in a meeting and have someone walk out and say, "That was the stupidest thing I ever heard." The irony is that, never in my life have I ever heard one of the guys talk about how stupid the ideas were. They always talk about the one idea that everybody liked and they agreed on. We leave the meeting and say, "I can't believe it." We need to leave the meeting saying, "Wow, they liked my idea and we're going ahead."

And finally — I think this is important for all of us — we have to learn to love what we do if we want to be brilliant. And we have to learn how to laugh. Nobody wants to play the game with somebody that takes it so seriously that they anguish all day and all week about every mistake. It's a game, gang. It really is a game. And we need to learn to love it if we're going to win.

Jane Fonda

Jane Fonda is well known for her stage and screen acting, but now, as an Atlanta resident, she focuses much of her time and energy on community service. She is the chair of the Georgia Campaign for Adolescent Pregnancy Prevention (G-CAPP), a statewide effort to reduce adolescent pregnancy rates through community, youth and family development, sustainable economic development and legislative activity.

Fonda established the Jane Fonda Center for Adolescent Reproductive Health at the Emory School of Medicine. Her gift will also endow a faculty chair, the Marion Howard Chair in Adolescent Reproductive Health, in the Department of Gynecology and Obstetrics at the school. In 2000, she joined with Georgia State University's Center for Excellence in Urban Education to form the Atlanta Partnership for Arts in Learning. She also serves as a trustee and vice president of the Turner Foundation and is a trustee of the Carter Center.

Fonda is the mother of Vanessa Vadim and Troy Garity.

JANE FONDA

...A LITTLE BIT ABOUT GIRLS

Jane Fonda to the YWCA of Greater Atlanta's Women of Achievement Luncheon

Atlanta — May, 2001

This really is a great honor. I feel like I'm part of a tremendous sisterhood here, not just the women up on the dais, but those sword- or phallic-symbol-wielding women that created the arch that I walked through and all of the other women in here. If they dropped a bomb on this building right now, we'd be losing a lot of testosterone. You're great. This is a tremendous honor. I love the Y. I want to just talk a little bit about girls.

In another one of my lives when I lived in California with another husband named Tom Hayden, who some of you know, we ran a children's camp for 15 years. And there was a young girl that went to that camp. It was an interesting camp. It had rich kids, poor kids, across the racial socio-economic spectrum. There was a young girl from a very disadvantaged background. She came from the ghetto in Oakland. And I became her mentor. She is now my daughter.

She would come back every year to the camp and it was clear that it had a big effect on her. I asked her once, "What was it about this camp that had such an effect on you?" She hesitated for a minute and she said, "Well, it was the first time that I'd ever met people who talked about the future." This was a very important eye-opening moment for me.

As an upper-middle-class woman, I realized that I had taken it for granted that all young people think about the future and ask themselves what they want to be when they grow up. And I learned that we can't assume that all young people think about that. Poor children, children who have been disadvantaged, abused, neglected, don't think in these terms. It takes good mentoring and programs like those delivered by the YWCA that can give girls back their sense of a future.

And there's another statement that I like to think about and quote a lot. It's by Marian Wright Edelman, founder of the Children's Defense Fund. She said, "Hope is the best contraceptive." And as someone — like many of you — who is concerned about the high rate of adolescent pregnancy, this is an important concept to internalize. "Hope is the best contraceptive." Again, that's something that the YWCA addresses, trying to give young people hope.

As I've been working in the field of adolescent pregnancy for the last six years in Georgia, and especially over the last few months when the issue of girl prostitutes in our city of Atlanta has been so much in the headlines, and because Nina Hickson is here and because Glenda Hatchett is here, it's something that hopefully we've all been thinking a lot about.

Society runs a great risk by scapegoating prostitutes and teenage mothers. Instead, we need to approach the problem with understanding and compassion, seeking ways to break the cycle.

Something that has dismayed me is the extent to which many people — some of whom should know better — tend to blame the girls, not just prostitutes, but girls who get pregnant, girls who get in trouble. We demonize them. We tend to assume that girls have considerable autonomy over their lives, their lives in general and their sex lives in particular. But instead of demonizing young mothers and prostitutes, we need to recognize that their behavior is not always an expression of their free will. In the area of sexuality, for instance, some studies show that 60 percent or more of mothers 15 years and younger have been sexually abused. The victims averaged 10-years-old at the time of the abuse, and the abusers averaged 27-years-old, and were very often members of the family or close family friends. Childhood sexual abuse was the single biggest predictor of teenage pregnancy over the last 40 years. According to a 1995 survey of 3,400 adult Americans done by sociologists at the University of Chicago, when a girl has been sexually abused, she's been brainwashed. Her sense of self, her sense of ownership of and control over her body, her capacity for self-efficacy has been taken away.

The question, "Who am I?" is answered, "I am someone who exists to please others." What Oprah Winfrey, herself a victim of rape and violence, calls *the disease to please*. For all these girls the demand to just say no is anathema. When has saying no had any impact on the way people treat them? A pregnant teenager may have had to have sex to please a man she depends on financially. She may fail to use contraception because the man either objects to it, or makes it difficult by complaining that it reduces his pleasure, or he may threaten violence.

Even for middle class girls like me who have not been abused, it's not so easy to look out for themselves. Our culture portrays sexually active girls as loose or cheap, thereby inhibiting girls from seeking information or services such as contraception, for fear that this would acknowledge that they want to or plan on having sex. A boy who carries a condom is a good boy, always prepared, like a Boy Scout; but a girl who carries a condom is a loose girl, who's "looking for it." It's okay if she gets drunk or is taking drugs and gets carried away in the spur of the moment. That's more forgivable than a girl who carries a condom and plans ahead. That's a gender bias in our culture that puts girls at tremendous risk. Often, girls are unable or unwilling to negotiate condom use because they've been taught by our culture to be docile and to please the man at all costs. Or they fear accusations of unfaithfulness or intimidation, especially when partners are several years older.

When our culture forbids girls to own their voice of desire or prepare in the event that there may be a sexual act performed, they're put at great risk. Sex becomes something they do to please someone else without any embodiment of their own pleasure. There's little consequence in giving away what you don't value or acknowledge. Society runs a great risk by scapegoating prostitutes and teenage mothers. Instead, we need to approach the problem with understanding and compassion, seeking ways to break the cycle, making it easier for young mothers to stay in school, helping them to develop tools for good parenting, providing them with caring mentors and programs which build their sense of self-worth, programs like the YWCA provides. So I am very, very honored to be brought into the wonderful circle of outstanding women honored by the YWCA of Greater Atlanta. I thank you very much.

Renée Lewis Glover

Renée Lewis Glover is the chief executive director of the Housing Authority of the City of Atlanta (AHA). The AHA provides market-competitive, affordable housing through the development of mixed-income, economically viable communities; operation of assisted communities; and administration of the housing choice voucher program in Atlanta.

In 2001, Glover received the Jesse O. Thomas Community Service Award from The Atlanta Urban League and the Atlanta Business League's highest award. She is president of the board of directors of the Council of Large Public Housing Authorities (CLPHA) and is a member of the National Advisory Council of Fannie Mae.

In November 2000, Glover received a congressional appointment to the Millennial Housing Commission. The Commission is charged with making recommendations to the U.S. Congress for legislation and policy governing the production, preservation and delivery of affordable housing.

DIVERSE COMMUNITIES OF HOPE
Renée Lewis Glover to the Atlanta Action Forum
Atlanta — July, 2001

Atlanta has given our nation many wonderful gifts, and one of them is a lesson in healing old racial wounds. No Southern city has done such a remarkable job of moving beyond the Jim Crow South. Atlanta has grown because of its ability to heal. It has prospered because of its citizens' ability to embrace their diversity.

And there's another example of diversity that we can model for America: a diversity of community, a blending of people of different socio-economic backgrounds, even in the very same neighborhoods. Atlanta has an opportunity to integrate the poor into the larger society, to actually have the affluent live among the impoverished, and for both groups to learn from one another. We have an opportunity to build communities that transcend race and class and income, communities that truly embrace and celebrate the diversity of our citizens.

Diversity usually means bringing women and minorities into meaningful positions in government and industry. We've worked hard for racial diversity, and we know its benefits. Diversity helps destroy myths and stereotypes. Coming in contact with people of different races teaches us that there is a fundamental common ground on which we all stand. Diversity teaches that no matter our color or religion, gender or nationality, we're all children of God, and we all have something useful to offer our society. It's been a powerful lesson that continues to help reshape our society.

While we have put our main focus, and understandably so, on racial and gender diversity, we haven't done the same with income diversity. Entire neighborhoods and schools are still stratified by income and class. The rich live "up there," the poor "down there." Rarely do the poor have an opportunity to rub shoulders with and learn from the affluent or middle classes.

And yet, all of the wonderful benefits we've derived from racial diversity can also be derived from socio-economic diversity. Through contact with those of different economic status, the affluent might learn that the poor aren't poor in spirit, in ambition or promise or intellect. The poor might gain from learning that the affluent are very much like themselves, with fears and goals and worries.

We need to begin to discover that just as there are powerful benefits gained from racial diversity, there is so much we can also derive from income diversity, diversity of neighborhoods, of the poor and non-poor living side by side.

Despite the naysayers who told us it wasn't possible, we at the Atlanta Housing Authority have discovered that it's possible to progress from diversity of race to diversity of income. With our private sector partners, we have transformed six rundown, dangerous and distressed Atlanta housing projects that used to warehouse only the poor, and developed them into beautiful, vibrant and safe mixed-income, mixed-use communities where the poor and the non-poor are neighbors, friends and allies. And we've seen that, just like with racial diversity, the benefits of income diversity are immeasurable.

The first and obvious benefit is that the poor are no longer isolated from the rest of society. There are few things more harmful to poor Atlantans than being herded together in veritable plantations for the poor. But that's what our old housing projects essentially did: They cut poor people off from the rest of society. Our nation's housing policies said: If you are poor and need assistance, go live over there with others just like you.

And what did those places turn into? Havens for drug-dealing, not for child-rearing. Violent places where children were killed in the line of fire by warring thugs and drug peddlers.

What message do we send our city's low-income children, who are so full of hope and promise, when we herd them off to such places? They probably pick up on the message that they've been cast aside. That the larger society considers them unworthy of joining in its prosperity. And what message do we send to their parents? That we will penalize their poverty with isolation for themselves, their children, their children's children.

One of the first benefits from mixed-income communities, therefore, was tearing down the warehouses for the poor and putting an end to all the ills that festered in them.

But we've discovered so many more benefits. Low-income families now have affluent neighbors who can help them appeal for better schools and prompt city services and more retail amenities. Their communities are no longer violent and rundown. Golf balls replace gunshot; master baths replace leaking toilets; a pristine play area replaces a dirt field littered with drug trash. Rebuilt communities such as the villages of East Lake and Centennial Place attract investment and new businesses, restaurants and jobs. Poor children are no longer herded into inferior schools. In fact, at both the villages of East Lake and Centennial Place, there are new elementary schools to serve neighborhood schoolchildren.

We need to begin to discover that just as there are powerful benefits gained from racial diversity, there is so much we can also derive from income diversity, diversity of neighborhoods, of the poor and non-poor living side by side.

And just as racial diversity teaches us more about other races, mixed-income communities are giving Atlantans new opportunities to learn about people from different socio-economic backgrounds. The poor are no longer segregated and isolated: They now have neighbors with resources and influence, people who can help steer them toward a job or a training program at their place of employment.

But every advancement has its cost, and there are costs associated with mixed-income housing. One cost is that there is less housing reserved exclusively for low-income residents. Another is that all residents – including low-income residents – must live up to higher standards of maintaining their homes and families. And still another *cost* is that property values can increase dramatically in rebounding communities, causing economic challenges for long-time residents and even prompting unfounded charges of "gentrification."

Some critics claim these costs outweigh the benefits – that, for instance, we ought to have more housing units reserved for the poor, even if they are substandard. But that's an argument for keeping the poor warehoused and isolated, for building communities readily identified by class and income, and for abandoning diversity. It is not surprising to find people arguing against income diversity, just as some argued against racial diversity. Both are mistaken.

And critics are mistaken in thinking that low-income families have less available housing. Many of the units previously reserved for the poor were uninhabitable. They were so rundown and decrepit that no one could live in them. Moreover, we ensured that all of the residents of our former projects received housing assistance through new, rebuilt housing or through the Section 8 program. Section 8 gives vouchers to low-income residents to spend on housing wherever they choose. Section 8 gives many residents, for the first time in their lives, a choice in housing. And many of them are choosing, not surprisingly, to live outside of subsidized housing, to move to the suburbs or to move closer to jobs and other opportunities.

New living standards imposed on all residents are another of the presumed costs of mixed-income housing. But this *cost* is actually a tremendous benefit, because it lifts low-income residents to the same standards we all must live by. For instance, if you rent a private apartment on Peachtree Street, certain standards will be required: that you pay your rent on time; that you do not allow outsiders to inhabit your apartment, and that you maintain the property in a reasonable condition. By asking low-income residents to abide by a similar set of standards, we send an empowering, uplifting message that tells them they are equally valuable members of society. Far from being onerous, the standards are uplifting. They give people faith in themselves. As one resident said, "Thank you for believing in me."

Finally, some critics complain that by building mixed-income communities, we are "gentrifying" neighborhoods, or displacing the poor to make room for the affluent. But the argument falls short because the very intent of mixed-income communities is to include everyone, and to exclude no one.

Of course, spruced-up neighborhoods, improved schools and new and convenient retail outlets bring greater housing prices, but what is the alternative? That the poor remain isolated in rundown and dangerous neighborhoods? That we leave low-income communities just as they are – for fear that improving them could increase property values? One housing resident reported that for 17 years she slept in her bathtub because she was afraid of the gunfire outside her bedroom window. Hopefully, that isn't the kind of neighborhood anyone thinks we should return to.

Atlanta was on the cutting edge in fostering racial diversity. New surveys tell us that our city is more racially integrated than the large metropolises of the North. That's a tribute to Atlanta and to the South. But we can't rest on our laurels. We have to embrace new forms of diversity. And just as we have learned and prospered from racial diversity, income diversity can deliver wonderful dividends.

Diversity works. Racial diversity works. Income diversity works. Let's give it a chance to work in our communities.

Sara J. González

Sara J. González is president of the Georgia Hispanic Chamber of Commerce, an organization committed to promoting the economic development of Hispanic businesses and individuals and to serving as a link between non-Hispanic entities and the Hispanic market.

González was instrumental in the passage of the Georgia Legislature's House Bill 607, which recognized Hispanics as a minority in Georgia. She was appointed by Governor Roy E. Barnes to the 2000 Census Count Committee and to the Governor's Commission of Hispanic Affairs.

González received *Women Looking Ahead* magazine's Ordinary Women with Extraordinary Talents Award and was named one of "Georgia's Most Powerful and Influential Women" by *Atlanta Magazine* in 2000. In 2001, the *Atlanta Business Chronicle* named González one of the 100 Most Influential Atlantans.

González also represents the Hispanic business community on several area boards.

LATINOS HAVE EARNED RESPECT FROM GEORGIA

*Sara J. González to the Legislative Session,
University of Georgia (Excerpts)*

Athens, Georgia — February, 2001

Latinos and Georgia's political leaders have not been playing on the same team.

This is hurtful and has to change. It has to change because the Latino work force and the number of Latino businesses in Georgia have been expanding rapidly. It has to change because our contributions to the economy of Georgia and to the tax base are very significant and growing. The Latino community is going to support with their votes and with their economic power those government and business leaders who work with us to make our state a better place for all.

The Hispanic Chamber of Commerce estimates that the Latino population of Georgia is nearing half a million. In the Atlanta metro area alone, we think there may be more than 250,000 Latinos. These are preliminary estimates that we expect will be confirmed by the 2000 census.

We also think that census figures will show that Georgia now ranks 16th among states in Latino population.

The Latino community is going to support with their votes and with their economic power those government and business leaders who work with us to make our state a better place for all.

Some sectors of Georgia's economy, such as agriculture, construction, poultry, carpet and landscaping would be severely affected if the Latino labor force were to abandon our state.

But in Georgia, the Latinos are not just doing the labor nobody else wants to do. The Latino population in Georgia has a higher level of education than the nation as a whole. Managers, professionals and armed forces personnel represent an unusually large portion of the Latino work force.

We don't have the latest figures yet, but in 1997, the median household income for Georgia Latinos was $30,000.

> *Those of us who have been here for a long time are using our knowledge, our resources and connections to ensure that all segments of Georgia society see Latinos as the asset they really are to the economy and culture of the state.*

We estimate that Latino-owned business in Georgia generates more than a billion dollars in receipts and employs more than 18,000 workers.

Ten Georgia Latino businesses are in the top 500 list of the largest Latino businesses in the nation, with total annual revenues of approximately $285 million.

Right now in Georgia, there are between 10,000 and 13,000 Latino-owned businesses.

In the last five years, without doing a membership drive, the business membership of the Georgia Hispanic Chamber of Commerce has grown by 415 percent. Our state is ranked fourth in the nation in the rate of growth of Latino buying power.

All indications are that the growth in Latino population, Latino business ownership and Latino buying power will continue for the foreseeable future.

Those of us who have been here for a long time are using our knowledge, our resources and connections to ensure that all segments of Georgia society see Latinos as the asset they really are to the economy and culture of the state.

It is about time we get the recognition we have earned with our hard work and with our investments of effort and capital into businesses that produce for all Georgians.

It is about time we get respect.

Beverly L. Hall

Dr. Beverly L. Hall is the superintendent of the Atlanta Public Schools. The school system has an active enrollment of nearly 57,000 students attending a total of 97 schools.

Hall is a member of the advisory board of the Harvard Urban Superintendents Program and serves as a mentor superintendent to participants in the doctoral program. She received The Brooklyn College Distinguished Achievement Award in 2000 from the Brooklyn College Alumni Association and the Year 2000 Diva Award from Atlanta's *Business to Business* Magazine for recognition as one of Atlanta's most dynamic women in business and public affairs.

Hall was born in Jamaica, W.I. and migrated to the United States after high school. She and her husband, Luis, have one son, Jason.

THE LONG VIEW
Beverly Hall to the Atlanta Foundation Forum (Excerpts)
Atlanta — September, 2000

Today, my task is to share with you the view of partnerships and collaboration from the perspective of the Atlanta Public Schools, and from where I sit as superintendent, that view is always the long view.

For education/business partnerships to be truly effective, they must be grounded in the long view of what is best for all the children. Donations, gifts and fund-raisers are fine, and they all have their places. But more than that, solid, long-term commitments and not one-time deals are what is needed to help overhaul public schools in Atlanta, and nationwide.

Middle-class families always supplement the amount per pupil allocated by taxpayers. They or their communities provide tutors, opportunities for organized sports and recreation, travel to other cities and countries, and all the resources to enrich their children's learning experiences. Poor children must have these same kinds of additional opportunities and resources to master the higher-level content that is required for them to work and live in this new Information Age. And we will need financial resources and expertise to compete with other school systems for the best and brightest professional staff and to invest in their continuous development to ensure that they have the knowledge and skills to teach all children at high levels.

However, our greatest challenge will be to work together to design a support system for children and families to address the non-academic barriers that prevent so many students from experiencing academic success.

Businesses have always helped schools, either as individual entities or through participation in Adopt-A-School or partnership programs. Through these types of initiatives, the private sector has often provided rewards for incentive programs: computers, funds for field trips, materials and supplies. And all of these are important, but as I stated earlier, they do not represent the kind of comprehensive, sustained partnership needed to significantly impact the lives and, in turn, the achievement levels of large numbers of students struggling to succeed despite the pervasive conditions of poverty with which they must contend every day.

There is a term familiar to all nursery school teachers called *parallel play*. Educational lecturer Roland Barth used this example to explain the term: Two 4-year-olds are busily engaged in opposite corners of a sandbox. Jimmy has a shovel and a bucket; Susan is playing with a rake and a hoe. At no time does Jimmy use Susan's rake or hoe, nor does Susan borrow Jimmy's bucket or shovels. Left alone, do they build a sandcastle together? They may inadvertently throw sand in each other's face from time to time but seldom do they interact. Although in close proximity for long periods of time and having much to offer one another, each works and plays pretty much in isolation.

This example of preschoolers at play captures the essence of why education/business partnerships have usually been less effective than either party had hoped. The isolation and fragmentation that result from our functioning in these parallel universes prevent us from developing the kinds of partnerships that can sustain the growth and development of ongoing, integrated support systems that can actually change children's lives for the better over the long term.

Kanter identifies three qualities of strong business alliances that I believe must also define the new relationship that must exist to move education/business collaborations to the next level. First, they must yield benefits for the partners, but they must be more than just a deal. They must be living systems that evolve progressively in their possibilities. Beyond the immediate reasons they have for entering into a relationship, the connection should offer the parties an option on the future, opening new doors and unforeseen opportunities. Second, alliances that both partners ultimately deem successful should involve creating new value together rather than mere exchange, getting something back for what you put in. Partners value the skills each brings to the alliance. Third, they cannot be controlled by formal systems, but require a dense web of interpersonal connections and internal infrastructures that enhance learning.

I realize that the old relationship based on business giving something to schools is easier, and it is still important. The problem, however, is that this type of partnership does not impact the most destructive and pervasive conditions of poverty that literally or figuratively destroy our children, because these forces are not exclusively material in nature.

For example, the number of words per hour the average 1- or 2-year-old child in a professional family hears at home is 2,153; in a working-class family, it's 1,251; in a family receiving federal/state welfare benefits, it's 616. The limited interaction with adults in the home setting experienced by poor children has a significant, detrimental impact on their learning years before they even enter kindergarten.

A traditional partnership where a business might provide books to a kindergarten class in a school in a poor neighborhood is not an effective intervention to stop or reverse the damage caused early in the lives of these children. A different type of partnership between the private sector, social service agencies and the public schools is needed to design the kinds of preschool initiatives that would allow children caught in these circumstances to enter school ready to learn.

One of the most powerful books that I have ever read is *A Framework for Understanding Poverty* by Dr. Ruby K. Payne. I will be forever indebted to the insight that I gained about the complex and consuming nature of the conditions that shape the behaviors, attitudes and beliefs of youth and adults who must navigate through life without the internal and external resources required to do so successfully. Too often we think of poverty merely as the absence of money. But I think all of us know people who were poor and, in some cases, we might have been ourselves without money at some point in our lives. Yet we were able to overcome this financial obstacle and go on to become productive adults.

What we often fail to recognize is that we had other resources that were even more valuable than money alone in shaping our paths. We had strong families, neighbors who were role models, teachers who stood in the gap for us. We may not have had middle-class money, but we had middle-class values, language and thought patterns that allowed us to successfully interpret and benefit from the institutions of our society.

It is imperative that we understand the vast difference between the kinds of partnerships necessary to help a student or a family when poverty results from circumstances and events that are often temporary in nature, and those support systems necessary to help free tens of thousands of students to reach their full potential by helping them to liberate themselves from the culture of poverty that develops over generations.

> *Children who live in a culture of poverty have role models, but they are frequently negative ones. Young people learn to live emotionally, spiritually and intellectually productive lives by watching and mimicking their adult role models.*

If the purpose of the partnership is the latter, the support system must include a full range of resources, not just financial ones. One goal of such a partnership might be to ensure that every child who needs a mentor has one. Children who live in a culture of poverty have role models, but they are frequently negative ones. Young people learn to live emotionally, spiritually and intellectually productive lives by watching and mimicking their adult role models. If positive mentors do not live in children's homes or communities, but are essential to understanding and functioning in the world, then those of us responsible for and committed to their well-being must design a system that provides them.

Schools, businesses and other institutions operate on middle-class norms, habits and traditions. But children whose primary culture is poverty do not know these rules.

To successfully address this problem, an effective partnership would need to create a process to help these children become bicultural so that they can survive in their world while transitioning to the larger one.

Sixty-four percent of the students served by the Atlanta Public Schools qualify for free or reduced-priced meals. Lack of money is a real issue for them and their families. And the negative impact of concentrated poverty in poor, urban schools is tremendous. Thus, the real challenge for those of us charged with leading institutions in our community is to create and then sustain the types of systemic alliances that will address all of the forces that contribute to the culture of poverty that suffocates the minds, bodies and spirits of too many of our children.

The Masai tribe are said to be the most fierce warriors throughout all of Africa. Interestingly, they greet each other not with, "Hello," "How are you?" or "How goes the life of a warrior?" — but with the question, "How are the children?" They wisely know that if the children are well, all is well. They know that the well-being of the community's children translates into the prosperity of the tribe as a whole.

And so the question which we must answer is: How are the children of Atlanta? Our work will not be completed until, together, we have created the types of partnerships and support systems that will allow us to honestly respond, "They are alive and well, each and every one."

Anne Harper

Dr. Anne Harper represented the fourth educational district on the Atlanta Board of Education from 1994 to 2001. During two terms in office, she served as vice president of the board for two years and chaired the Board Standards, Superintendent Search, Student Performance and Strategic Planning committees.

Harper founded the Coalition for Gender Equity in Sports and was the catalyst behind Georgia's Equity in Sports Act (2000). She serves on the board of directors of Girls On The Run of Atlanta and Cool Girls Inc. She was named a YWCA Woman of Achievement in 1995 and is a Leadership Atlanta graduate. She co-chairs the Georgia Women's Movement Project advisory board at Georgia State University and is first vice president of the board of the NOW Legal Defense and Education Fund in New York, NY.

A graduate of Smith College with a doctorate in political science from the University of Michigan, Harper leads an independent consulting practice, Harper Consulting, specializing in strategic planning, organizational development and communication. She and her husband, Greg Nobles, have two daughters, Phoebe and Sarah.

WOMEN & POWER: CHOOSING TO LEAD

*Anne Harper to Spelman College students,
faculty and guests (Excerpts)*

Atlanta — March, 2001

On June 27, 1987, Angela Davis opened the National Women's Studies Association Conference with a keynote speech entitled *Lifting As We Climb*. Davis called for the women assembled at Spelman College on that hot June day to embrace the principle employed by black women in the club movement: lift as we climb. Davis exhorted her audience to "… climb in such a way as to guarantee that all of our sisters, regardless of social class, and indeed all of our brothers, climb with us. This must be the essential dynamic of our quest for power — a principle that must not only determine our struggles as Afro-American women, but also govern all authentic struggles of dispossessed people."

I want to suggest to you that Davis was defining an important difference in the way women and other minority people can choose to lead: We can choose to lead based on power sharing rather than power grabbing. We can choose to lead based on building power with others instead of power over others. We can choose to empower ourselves and others who have not had opportunities to fulfill their dreams, rather than gain power for ourselves alone.

Oxygen Media has provided us with some survey research statistics indicating that many American women express an aversion to power and are often not particularly supportive of other women in positions of power. Sixty-five percent of survey respondents say women often resent or are jealous of powerful women, while 55 percent say that women with power tend to be difficult to deal with. Of the 86 percent of women who have had a female boss, only 43 percent said they liked that situation. Many women (52 percent) think other women judge female politicians more harshly than male politicians. Only 9 percent say that they would support a woman candidate because she is female, but when tested, many women do in fact favor women candidates.

I think it is no great mystery why women are reluctant to seek power for themselves or to admire other women who do so. Power in most human communities is associated with exercising influence or control over others. And having the ability to act or produce effects on others derives all too often from privilege based on wealth, skin color or gender. Power as we know it in our society is almost always, in the end, about promoting or enriching yourself. *Taking care of number one* is the way people in the business world began to put it a decade or so ago.

> *What does it take for women to gain and exercise power in a representative democracy? First, women must have voice. They must have the words to express their needs and aspirations, and they must find a way to raise those voices so that they can be heard and understood by those around them.*

Often women, having experienced oppression based on gender, race or wealth, are not quick to embrace the exercise of power over others. They sometimes hesitate to climb to the top of the organizational pyramid. Does this derive from their sense of responsibility for the weakest members of society, the children, the sick and the elderly? Perhaps women are operating from a greater sense of obligation to others. That may be in fact what led to the concept of "lifting as we climb." Women want to bring others along with them on the journey to a better life. They want to lift their families and neighbors up with them as they ascend to greater heights.

Of course, there are notable women throughout history who have not shied away from holding and exercising power in the least. I will not elaborate here on the many famous queens to powerful queens. But I think we can say that most of these renowned female leaders were exceptional in their day, and they came into power through the institution of monarchy, inheriting their positions through familial privilege.

Democracies, both ancient and modern, have been less frequent to choose women leaders, although parliamentary democracies in Europe and occasionally Asia have been ahead of the United States in choosing women heads of state.

What does it take for women to gain and exercise power in a representative democracy? First, women must have voice. They must have the words to express their needs and aspirations, and they must find a way to raise those voices so that they can be heard and understood by those around them.

Our foremothers in the suffrage movement knew this well. They explicitly expressed their plans to raise their voices in the Declaration of Sentiments in 1848:

"In entering upon the great work before us, we anticipate no small amount of misconception, misrepresentation and ridicule; but we shall use every instrumentality within our power to effect our object. We shall employ agents, circulate tracts, petition the state and national legislature, and endeavor to enlist the pulpit and the press in our behalf." (Declaration of Sentiments, Seneca Falls, 1848)

Today, women have gone far beyond tracts and petitions and have published their words of protest and vision in every imaginable vehicle available, including the current crop of electronic media. When not able to influence the owners of "the pulpit and the press," we have created our own pulpits and presses — and Internet companies.

Voice and courage must be accompanied by a willingness to reach out to other people in all their diversity and create common understandings; in short, we must engage in "coalition politics." Spelman alum Dr. Bernice Johnson Reagon explains it well when she says, "You don't go into coalition because you just like it ... coalition work is not work done in your home. Coalition work has to be done in the streets. And it is some of the most dangerous work you can do." But it is work that women have a history of doing at the grassroots level.

Women today do have the choice to lead in a wide variety of venues from business to politics, from religious institutions to community organizations. And we have a choice to lead in new ways, to bring others along with us in coalition and collaboration. Instead of exercising domination from a position of race or class privilege or engaging in manipulation from a position of oppression, women today are choosing to achieve their aspirations cooperatively with others, sharing resources and building bridges across the prejudices that too often divide diverse communities of interest.

Women have the opportunity today to redefine the way our society thinks about and uses power. Women who have worked collaboratively in their communities have the advantage of being comfortable with sharing information and responsibility. They are accustomed to sharing work and sharing credit.

One of my greatest pleasures is mentoring the next generation of women leaders. I urge all of the students in the audience to seek out opportunities to talk with the women leaders in your communities. Volunteer to work in political campaigns and government offices. Ask lots of questions and take on new responsibilities. Most of the women I know in appointed or elected positions want to hear from you and to work with you.

As students, you are still at an early stage of your life's journey. The education at a liberal arts college like Spelman is going to prepare you to choose some kind of community leadership over the course of your years. Former Spelman President Johnnetta Cole identified a contemporary liberal arts education as needing to be "worldcentric." By that term, she meant that education must be based on social awareness and responsibility, a broad knowledge of the diversity of cultures and participation in the lives of others through service.

You are learning the skills of thorough fact-gathering and thoughtful analysis, while broadening your horizons. All of these

> *Instead of exercising domination from a position of race or class privilege or engaging in manipulation from a position of oppression, women today are choosing to achieve their aspirations cooperatively with others, sharing resources and building bridges across the prejudices that too often divide diverse communities of interest.*

college experiences can help you prepare yourself to be comfortable with holding and exercising leadership positions across your lifetime. And they can prepare you to be comfortable with the leadership of other women — for we must all work harder to support one another. I urge you all to gain strength from our exchange of ideas today and to be fearless in choosing to lead in the future.

Nina R. Hickson

Nina R. Hickson serves as a judge of the Juvenile Court of Fulton County, presiding over legal matters involving children accused of delinquent activities as well as abused and neglected children.

Hickson helped found the Sister-to-Sister mentoring program, which involves the Georgia Association of Black Women Attorneys and first-time female offenders. She is a board member for the National Child Labor Committee, the Georgia Diversity Program of the State Bar of Georgia and Georgia Court Appointed Special Advocate Inc. She has also served on the advisory board of the Boys-to-Men Project and as the vice chair of the Delinquent Services Committee of the Georgia Council of Juvenile Court Judges.

Hickson has one daughter, Wesley Victoria.

IS THERE ANYTHING TOO HARD FOR GOD?
Nina R. Hickson to the congregation of Ben Hill United Methodist Church
Atlanta — July, 2000

This morning, I would like to introduce you to a 16-year girl named Alysia, who was born HIV positive to a crack-addicted mother. Placed in state custody at age 7 because her mother refused to learn how to care for her. Raped by her half-brother at age 8. Back in the state's care, she ran away. Her mother died when she was 12. Involved in prostitution at 12. She bore a child at 15, who was immediately placed in the state's care. In and out of juvenile detention.

I met her during her 28th contact with the juvenile justice system. She came before me on a shoplifting charge, and I committed her to the Department of Family and Children Services and the Department of Juvenile Justice with the hope she would get treatment for her many issues. After months of fighting with people who just wanted her locked up for the rest of her childhood, we finally got her a secure placement where she can be cared for and treated.

Looking at our text of Jeremiah 32:27, Jeremiah was one of the major prophets who lived during the final days of the Kingdom of Judah. Like Moses and Isaiah, he did not think he was worthy of this calling, but nonetheless obeyed God, who required him to warn God's people of the catastrophe that was to fall upon them because of their sin and idolatry.

In the 32nd chapter, we find Jeremiah being obedient to God in purchasing a field in a land that God promised to destroy. Also, true to his reputation as the "Weeping Prophet," he lamented about the sins of the people, God's judgment of them, and that God could ask him to buy land which was about to be taken and buried.

In response, God asks, "Is anything too hard for Me?"

You see, God directed Jeremiah to purchase this land as evidence of His intervention to restore His people. Can you imagine how people reacted to Jeremiah prophesying the destruction of Judah?

In fact, he was imprisoned and labeled a traitor as a result. But even after proclaiming that God would allow the Babylonians to take Judah, he goes and buys the very property he said God would destroy.

As with Jeremiah, sometimes when God gives us an assignment, it can be very difficult. Sometimes, it seems like a nonsense assignment.

Often God's assignment will require us to move out of our comfort zone. One of God's assignments that I believe that we as a community have not done well has to do with our children.

Back to Alysia, the 16-year-old I introduced you to earlier; I think she is indicative of how we as a community of believers have not been obedient in our assignment for God.

In Matthew 18:14, we are told that it is not the will of our Heavenly Father that any child should perish. And yet, right here in Fulton County, I see thousands of children treated as if they are expendable.

I see 7-year-olds who are rejected by their families; 10-year-olds with no supervision who become prostitutes; 13-year-olds who feel responsible for their younger siblings and their parents; babies born and abandoned in crack houses; and teenagers expected to take care of themselves.

Just as the people of Judah sacrificed their children to idols, we as a community are allowing children to be sacrificed when we fail to practice care and nurturing and when we allow the "chase for the dollar" to take precedence over teaching them values and letting them know that someone loves them.

I am not suggesting that those of us who have children are not doing the very best we can, but I am suggesting that we as a community of believers are not doing enough. At a minimum, we need to keep the children of our community lifted in prayer. But there are so many other things we can do: Letting them know they are loved; being a significant adult in a child's life; encouraging parents, especially single parents; coaching or mentoring parents (volunteering in after-school mentoring); insisting that our legislators make decisions which reflect that the care of families and children is more important than another prison or road project; becoming a member of Court Appointed Special Advocates or the Citizens Panel Review; and insisting prosecutors prosecute child abusers and exploiters.

Doing these things takes us out of our comfort zone. It requires sacrifice, it requires risking rejection and ridicule. But accepting "God-sized" assignments leads to a crisis of belief that requires us to act in faith and make adjustments in our lives.

The second characteristic of God that I see in this text is that God purifies. God was not pleased with Judah's disobedience and was going to purify his people and establish a new covenant. He was willing to wipe out an entire people and country to save the children from the corrupt influences of their parents and society.

While I am uncertain whether God would wipe out our entire generation because of our failure to obey his assignment regarding the children, I do believe He will allow the natural consequences of our disobedience to lead to the further "breaking down" of our communities.

However, if we choose to obey God and let Him order our steps, particularly as it relates to our children, I believe that He can do what I believe we see in Jeremiah 37-42.

The third and final point of this message is that God restores. God's restoration requires our cooperation and participation.

As you will recall, Alysia's story has not ended in despair, but with the hope of restoration. She is in a secure placement getting the care and attention needed to address the trauma. What she has experienced in her life, with God's help, will enable her to be a blessing to others.

God's restoration requires our doing what 2 Chronicles 7:14 requires of us: "If my people, who are called by my name, will humble themselves and pray and seek my face and turn from their wicked ways, then I will hear from heaven and will forgive their sin and will heal their land."

Even when His people are disobedient, God restores us. And so I ask — is anything too hard for God?

Patsy Jo Hilliard

Patsy Jo Hilliard has served as the first woman mayor of East Point, Ga., since 1993. She is also co-owner and executive officer of WASET Educational Production Company.

Hilliard serves on the board of directors of the NAACP Atlanta Chapter, Bridges Across Atlanta, South Fulton Senior Services and the Fulton County Council on Aging. She is a member of the Atlanta League of Women Voters and the Atlanta Chapter of Links Inc. She chaired the Trust Committee of the Fulton-DeKalb Hospital Authority, and she is a Docent Emeritus of the High Museum of Art. The Atlanta Business League named her One of the Top 100 Women of 2000.

Hilliard is married to Dr. Asa Hilliard III, and is the mother of four children: two sons, Asa IV and Hakim, and two daughters, Robi and Patricia. She has seven grandchildren.

PATSY JO HILLIARD

THE SECOND TRINITY: GOD, FAMILY & FRIENDS

Patsy Jo Hilliard to the Divine Unity Missionary Baptist Church, Family & Friends Day

East Point, Georgia — May, 2001

This is a good day. This is a happy time. Today, we are with family and friends, and love is in the air. This is somewhat of a reunion — a reunion with family, with friends and with God. I think of it as a Second Trinity.

You hear on the news all the time about how bad society has become. You're always told about the breakdown of the nuclear family. We're bombarded each day with negative information. It's almost enough to make you say, "Why bother?" In spite of all that, I want to tell you that I feel encouraged and blessed. We're all so blessed. We're blessed to be among those who love us no matter what — our family and our friends. And you know that if you don't feel loved by anyone else, you're still a child of God and that is an ever-present, everlasting, all-encompassing love.

Let me talk briefly about family. The dictionary describes family as a group of people of common ancestry. It can also be a group of people united under a common conviction or a common affiliation. But those definitions sound so clinical, so cut and dry. When I think of family, I think of love — unconditional love. I think of people who are there for you in the best of times and in the worst of times. I think of family as those who make you feel safe and supported no matter what heavy burdens life may place upon you.

It's the same feeling with friends, real friends. Friends aren't necessarily related to you by blood. But in a sense, friendship can be even more significant because friends are there for you by choice. What do friends do? Friends support each other. Friends are loyal to each other. Friends comfort each other. Friends encourage each other, just like family.

At a time when individuality reigns supreme, we need each other now more than ever. Our losses and our successes are not ours alone. We are nothing without family and friends, and we are nothing without God.

Therefore, it's important to keep our lives in perspective. For example, when someone wins a championship, when the award is put in their hands, she looks to the audience in search of family or friends to connect with in a moment of shared pride and glory. The award is nothing if you don't have someone to share in the joy with you.

By the same token, that person might not have been able to accomplish her goal without the support of family and friends encouraging her. And none of it would have been possible except through the grace of God. This is why I call the union of God, family and friends a Second Trinity. If we think of it in this way, there can be an even deeper appreciation for the sanctity of family, the value of friendship and the acceptance of a God-filled life. Understand that this is where we find our strength. And you can't put a dollar value on this kind of love. It is priceless, but it is free.

There's a story of a rich man who took his son out to the country to show him just how poor people can be. They spent a whole day and night at the farm home of a poor family. When they got back from their trip, the father wanted to know if his son now understood just how poor people can be. The boy assured him that he understood. The father asked him what he had learned. The son said, "We have a pool that reaches to the middle of the garden, they have a creek that has no end. We have imported lamps in the garden, they have the stars. Our patio reaches to the front yard, they have the whole horizon." When the boy was finished, the father was speechless. Then the boy added, "Thanks for showing me how poor we are!"

See, it all depends on how you look at life. If you have God, family and friends in your life, you have everything. You can have all the money in the world, but if you're poor in spirit, you have absolutely nothing. That's why we should cherish the people in our lives who help hold us up. I know that I am who I am because of God, my family and my friends, and I love them all dearly.

And where is the home of the Second Trinity? It is here. It is our church. The black church is the most enduring, stabilizing institution in the African-American community. It is like our mother. And since we're talking about family, I guess you can say the African-American church is akin to "Big Momma's" house. Just like our blood "Big Momma," our church has historically been our spiritual anchor and the main source of survival and progress.

Our church has been the central meeting place in times of need and change. From our church has come social revolution, politics, community and economic development, arts, music, education, civic associations, business enterprises and a wealth of other resources. From our church hails a rich spiritual tradition of survival and liberation emanating from our souls through song and sermon.

And just as our family home has been a place where we get our nurturing, so has our church given us an environment in which we can learn self-respect, group identity, social and public skills and the value and necessity of cooperation. The church, just like our family home, is where we shape our attitudes. The church, just like our family, has united us by a web of cultural, social and spiritual guidelines that help to keep us together in times of adversity and strife by giving us a sense of community.

Again, I say the church is our family, our mother, our home. Home is where we're born and where we want to die or be reborn. When we're at our lowest, we feel we can make it if we can just get back home. It's where our history is. It's where we can feel our ancestors whisper wisdom through the walls. It's where the food tastes better, the laughter is heartier, and the love is the mightiest. It's where a child can fall and scrape his leg, and with a kiss on the sore spot, it can be healed. It's where a child scribbles out his first undistinguishable picture and is praised for how beautiful it is. It's where you can talk about each other, but no one outside of the family better say anything bad about them. That's family. That's friendship. That's church. That's home. That's unconditional love. That's the God in us.

Alene Isaac

Alene Isaac is the director of grants and contracts accounting for Clark Atlanta University. She also serves as director of Christian education at St. Paul Missionary Baptist Church in East Point, Ga. In her work at St. Paul, she teaches classes and Bible studies, is a member of the ministerial staff and develops curriculum and course content for Bible studies in leadership, women's studies and new member orientation.

Isaac is a member of the National Council of University Research Administrators, the Society of Research Administrators and the American Association of University Women. She has been featured as a speaker at the National Baptist Convention of America, Young Women's Division and the First Annual Young Women's Conference in Houston, Texas.

THESE THREE: STAND BOLDLY, WALK HUMBLY AND FORGIVE
Alene Isaac to the congregation of Antioch Baptist Church
Waco, Texas — August, 1998

Once her beginning, the role of woman has been defined and redefined by so many, including herself. No doubt this is because of the many dynamics actively at work and at play, twenty-four/seven. Woman's role has been redefined so many times because of the additional responsibility required of her and accepted by her. Woman may be the only creature whose role has dramatically changed since the beginning.

Perhaps the harshest consequence of what occurred in the Garden, seemingly, was given to woman. We not only have pain in childbearing, but we also have to work by the sweat of our brow. I do not believe that was a part of the divine plan, at least not in the fashion that it is lived out today. Notwithstanding, because of *whose* we are, our growth and development as women have adapted to the culture and call of the times. We have embraced every challenge and worked to conquer every foe. We have done well, although there is still much to be done. Life sometimes seems unfair, but what is done is done, what needs to be done will be done, and whatever I need to do to get it done, I will do.

"These three" in the religious community often refer to faith, hope and love, and perhaps they are the foundation of The Three discussed here. We have an obligation to the generations before and behind us to examine not only the cause and legacy, but also what significant role each of us is to play, if we are willing to be more than spectators in this thing called life. If we dare come down from the balcony and take a closer look, we will find that too many of us view life through rose-colored glasses. When you come down from the balcony, when you come from outside in, when you scratch beyond the surface, you get a first-hand, close-up view. It is astounding. Once you've seen it, you must decide if The Three will become part of you, part of your character, your moral view.

What is it that I have seen? It is whatever economic, political, social, spiritual and moral circumstance you have encountered for that time or moment. What are you going to do with it, about it, to it, for it? More importantly, after your encounter, what, if anything, has it done to you? Action will be required. Make no mistake; you do decide, either by what you do or what you don't do, by what you say or what you don't say. Whether you are cognizant of it or not, every circumstance and situation in life gets processed through life — some focused and deliberate, some not.

There is reservation and requisition placed on the one who truly chooses to stand boldly, walk humbly and forgive amid the negative, ugly unpleasantness of life. "Truly chooses" would indicate that more than lip service and social conversation is involved. It is easy, my friends, to stand firm and bold in what you do and say when the majority, or a good bit of it — or even a reasonable portion of it — is standing with you. Every person should, at some point, open up their mind and heart and honestly ask the questions: Who am I and why am I? What is or has been my participation and contribution? Do the attributes that are currently a part of me and reflect what I have become resemble These Three? Maybe it would help if we asked ourselves what it means to stand boldly, walk humbly and forgive. What does it really mean?

To stand boldly requires uncommon, individual and independent — not interdependent — courage. If you can only be courageous when you have the support of others, examine yourself. That is not to say that those with whom we come in contact with do not influence the impact of one's decision. Life is not lived in a vacuum, but the decision, once made, should be original and it should be genuine — not copied, plagiarized, nor duplicated, but original. That means it must come from a place deep within oneself, where no one else has visited or lived but God. After your examination, always render your conclusion, your decision. My beloved, that takes courage. We must begin by first believing that what I am called to do in life (whatever the arena), only I can do. No one can do it for me. It is my appointment with time. Some of us have more appointments than others, but we all have them.

Sooner or later, life brings us face to face with that thing, that circumstance, that fact, that situation, that question, that destiny, and we must act. We must respond. Will we have the faith and courage at the time of the encounter to respond boldly, originally, genuinely and responsibly? Remember, you just may be standing alone. It is difficult to get along in this world sometimes. That is because most of us become more attached to the person of another rather than the ideas of another. Therefore, when it is time for our appointment with life, we find ourselves supporting people rather than ideas or rights. The right thing to do oftentimes gets lost in the equation of the relationship between two individuals. I think they call that politics. It also lands us between two opinions and most of us don't have the courage to separate the good idea or right idea from the individual.

It is important for us to respect others and be respected by them. My hat is off to the one who can "walk with kings and still have the common touch." Walking humbly keeps you in the posture for service. Service is required of all of us, those who number themselves among the great and those we call the common. We must each see the other as the great and believe that we all are the common. Walking humbly keeps a fine-tuned memory and a fine-tuned heart. When you search them, you find that there is still work yet undone. There is no *I have arrived*. Walking humbly keeps us from being pretentious and arrogant. Life teaches us that when we get to that place we think exists called, *I have arrived*, and find ourselves there alone or with one or two others, we should realize immediately that we must have taken a wrong turn somewhere along the away. What about the ones who were traveling with us? Did we get so caught up in what we were doing that we forgot why we were doing it and for whom?

> *It is important for us to respect others and be respected by them. My hat is off to the one who can "walk with kings and still have the common touch."*

In the multidimensional, multifaceted and multifocused life of a woman, there must be at least one avenue of escape. I say multi because woman is required to perform in many different capacities and she is expected to perform superbly. And we do. The avenue of escape is called forgiveness. No, it is not called a shopping spree. It is not called a long hot bath. It is not called dinner at a fine restaurant. It is not called women's rights or women's liberation or women's suffrage. All these things may have been born out of forgiveness. If you take a look back over the centuries, the evidence is everywhere; the debris is scattered all over the landscape of life. We could have chosen to pick it up and bring it along, but that would have only made a less peaceful world than we currently have.

Forgiveness is the tool of survival, sane survival. When we forgive, we liberate our offender and we liberate ourselves. Forgiveness lets me be uniquely me. It raises my value as a human being when I do it as it should be done, sincerely and genuinely. When we do not forgive, we become what the offense makes of us. We, in one way or another, become captives. But when we let go, when we release the offense and the violation, the offender and the violator, we open the door and the window of life so that the bright sunshine can come in. Clouds and darkness dissipate.

Liberation and freedom has nothing to do with physical location or anything material. Freedom is a state of mind and heart. In this freedom, one finds peace. Inner peace. Inner peace is a prerequisite of survival. Forgiveness is no small undertaking. I once heard someone say that "forgiveness is harder than dying." I believe that. Sometimes, what makes it hard is our concern for safeguarding our rights, so they are never again violated. God will safeguard them for us. We should exert more energy on learning how to forgive. There is no secret or mystery surrounding it. It is not something you contemplate. It is something you do, and you must do it. Therefore, it is better to make it a way of life. A forgiving spirit and a forgiving heart should be with you at all times, a part of your character. At no time should you be caught without it.

Forgiveness is the tool of survival, sane survival. When we forgive, we liberate our offender and we liberate ourselves.

Take your position, your station in life, whether it has been defined by you or by another and stand boldly, walk humbly and forgive. In the sunshine or in the rain, in the suburbs or the inner city ghetto, in the palace or the projects, in the workplace or in the home, among friends and enemies, among the learned and the unlearned, in peace and in war, in captivity and liberation, you will need These Three.

Ingrid Saunders Jones

Ingrid Saunders Jones is senior vice president of corporate external affairs for The Coca-Cola Company and chairperson of The Coca-Cola Foundation. In these roles, she directs the vision and involvement of The Coca-Cola Company in community, philanthropic and civic affairs and leads the company's philanthropic commitment to education.

Jones also chairs the board of directors for the United Way of Metropolitan Atlanta and is the immediate past chair of the Community Foundation of Greater Atlanta and the National Black Arts Festival. She serves on the boards of the Andrew Young School of Policy Studies at Georgia State University and the Desmond Tutu Peace Foundation, among others.

In recognition of her work and her contributions to civic and community causes, Jones has received the National Action Network's Keepers of the Dream Award, the YWCA of Greater Atlanta's Woman of Achievement Award and the NAACP Atlanta Chapter's Jondelle Johnson Legacy Award.

THE CARE OF A COMMUNITY
Ingrid Saunders Jones to the Sandy Springs Society (Excerpts)
Atlanta — September, 1999

I thought about the common thread that runs within your membership and that I share with you, and that common thread really is *community*. I want to thank you for the wonderful work you are doing for the Atlanta metropolitan community and for embracing the responsibility to care and act.

As individuals and as members of the Sandy Springs Society, you recognize that good citizens engage in the substance of their communities. The care of a community means paying attention to the small issues and also to the tough issues that demand hard decisions and effective action.

At The Coca-Cola Company, we believe responsible corporate citizens must also engage in quality-of-life issues in the community. One issue in particular is education — education of the nation's young people.

The Coca-Cola Company has made education our philanthropic focus, and we contributed more than $100 million during the 1990s. Education and having a well-trained and educated work force play a pivotal role in the ongoing success of The Coca-Cola Company.

Education has also played a pivotal role in my life. The importance of education is a concept that I grew up with, a concept my mother and father instilled in me beginning at an early age. It was this concept of education, knowledge, excellence and preparation that led to what I call my three careers: first career, being that of an educator and a non-profit advocate; second career, being in and learning about government service; and third career, the business sector and its responsibility to and relationship with the community.

First, a little bit about myself. My parents' singular influence was effectively augmented throughout my childhood by the words and wisdom of the strong caring women of my family. My mother has three sisters. Their combined ages, 84, 81 and 79, total 244 years. My grandmother lived until I was 25; my great-grandmother lived until I was 15.

I had the benefit of seeing and listening to a powerful group of women — my mother, her sisters, her mother and her mother's mother

— sitting on one of those wrap-around porches in the mountains of North Carolina. I learned a great deal from these remarkable women and their combined life's experiences. The times we shared are among my warmest and most wonderful memories.

One thing I remember vividly is hearing them say from time to time, "You have to live it to learn it." And, as you know, they were right! So let me share with you some of what I've lived and some of what I have learned, living and working and growing in different places and different times.

My father was born in Knoxville, Tenn. He is 85-years-old; he attended Knoxville College and the University of Michigan. My mother was born in Tryon, N. C. She is 84; she attended Knoxville College and went on to graduate with a degree from Wayne State University.

I was born and raised in Detroit, Mich., and attended the Detroit Public Schools. I was a good student, and I was active in high school sports. I truly understand the Nike commercial about the confidence that sports build in young women.

True personal freedom means that I can and will do what I know, in my head and in my heart, is right.

Without offering specifics about my age, suffice it to say that I am a child of the 1960s — an era we remember with a great deal of nostalgia. The truth of the matter is that those were turbulent times for our country and for our nation's young people.

So when the warm nostalgia of the Sixties flows to my ears in the music of the Beatles, Four Tops, the Rolling Stones, the Temptations, Aretha Franklin, the Supremes and others, I also remember John and Bobby, Medgar, Malcolm and Martin. And I recall the Vietnam War and the many challenges of the Civil Rights Movement. It took personal strength to live through that era for all of us, regardless of race, religion, politics or gender.

During those years and since, I have encountered many instances of social prejudice. I have dealt with people who regularly tried to make me invisible, sometimes because of the color of my skin, sometimes because of my gender, and sometimes for both reasons.

But I learned early in life that, as Eleanor Roosevelt wrote, "No one can make you feel inferior without your consent." That extraordinary First Lady was absolutely right. Another way to put it is to remember that "it's not what they call you, but rather what you answer to."

At such times, when I needed strength, I drew upon some very special wisdom my parents shared with me. My mother and father taught me by word and deed that:

"It's good to be afraid from time to time. But to live a life of true personal freedom, one has to be fearless."

I think about that wisdom often. And there are three questions I associate with my parents' words. First of all, "Why is it good to be afraid sometimes?"

Fear can be good when it tells us we are moving forward and growing, stretching and striving to pursue our goals in life. Anxiety is a signal that we are entering new territory, moving beyond yesterday's comfort zone and challenging ourselves.

The second question, as we move past yesterday's comfort zone, "What is a life of true personal freedom?"

Each of us has our own definition. But here is what true personal freedom means to me: True personal freedom means that I can and will do what I know, in my head and in my heart, is right. True personal freedom defies the limitations placed on us by the unkind forces of society. And most of all, true personal freedom mitigates the limitations we often place on ourselves. It mitigates the boundaries that we sometimes build around ourselves, boundaries such as uncertainty, pessimism and self-doubt.

And, my third question, "What does it mean to be fearless?"

To be fearless does not mean moving with a blind disregard for danger, for many of life's dangers are very real.

On the contrary, to be fearless means knowing that there is far less danger in working for what you believe in than there is in passively surrendering to, what I call, the other side: the side that keeps us from taking what "is" as we know it today and making it "better" and "best" for tomorrow.

Tomorrow, of course, is beyond our knowing.

So the appropriate response to the future is to prepare for it today to the best of our ability. Such preparation is another key lesson that I have learned along the way.

When I was growing up, I had no notion whatsoever that one day I might become a senior executive at The Coca-Cola Company. In fact, at that time, the only impression I had of the company was its great soft drinks, especially ice-cold Coca-Cola on a hot summer day in Motown.

And now, nearly 17 years later, as I look back over my three careers, I see clearly the importance of being well prepared and taking calculated risks in life. And I know that I learned important lessons in each workplace along the way.

Teaching school enhanced my appreciation for the importance of our children. It reminded me that all children are our children and that we all have a role in raising every child. Of course, never can we supplant the essential role of the parent, but neither can we forget that every child truly is the future we share.

In a similar fashion, serving in Atlanta city government refined my understanding of the role of governance and the democratic process and the importance of coalition-building. I came to understand how people with different backgrounds and diverse views can reach agreement on common goals and work together to achieve them.

My business experience has expanded my awareness of the role of responsible corporate citizenship in our society. I understand that corporations can and must make a difference in the communities in which they do business and in the society of which they are a part. In fact, my past career assignments often influence my present-day decision-making in one way or another.

As I mentioned earlier, the women of my family used to tell me that you have to "live it to learn it." That makes experience essential to learning, just as learning is essential to life. But, of course, decisions are not always based entirely, or even primarily, on experience. Another component of my decision-making throughout the years is the role of what I call "a greater force."

Each of us, during life's journey, is faced with moments of destiny — the times when one simple action can bring a new world of change, risk, potential and possibility. That's called faith.

Faith helps us to take risks and to see ourselves connected to our communities and the world. This is where the notion of service and being a servant leader comes from. Indeed, more than anything else in this life, service to one another connects us with one another.

But, of course, you, the women of the Sandy Springs Society, already know this. That is why you continue to reach out to enhance the lives of others — from preschoolers to senior citizens — from refugees in Oklahoma to refugees in Kosovo. As homemakers and career professionals, as wives and mothers and grandmothers, as women who care, you give generously of your time, talents and treasuries to assist those in need, to shape a better future for all people in our community.

When I consider the contributions of your organization, I am reminded of the essential role that women have played in every society since the dawn of human history. I am reminded of the words of that great educator, Mary McCleod Bethune, who said:

"Next to God, we are indebted to women, first for life itself and then for making it worth living."

So, as you reach out to serve our community, take pride in the fact that you are helping to write the "future history" of Atlanta, even as you carry on the best traditions of the past.

It is what we, you and I, do today that truly writes the history of tomorrow, and we must write that history with intention and purpose!

Monica Kaufman

Monica Kaufman, WSB-TV's 5, 6 and 11 p.m. Action News anchor, joined the Channel 2 staff in August 1975. The University of Louisville graduate was a reporter with *The Louisville Times* for four years. She worked in public relations for Brown-Forman Distillers before joining WHAS-TV in Louisville as a reporter and anchor for two years.

Kaufman has received numerous awards, including 23 local and Southern Regional Emmy Awards for Talent, Reporting and "Monica Kaufman Closeups." In 1995, she was awarded first place recognition for Excellence in Journalism/Documentary by the Atlanta Chamber of the Society of Professional Journalists for "Hot Flash! The Truth about Menopause." The documentary also won two National American Women in Radio and Television Commendation awards.

Kaufman is a member of various professional organizations, including The Society of Professional Journalists, Sigma Delta Chi, The National Association of Black Journalists, The Atlanta Association of Black Journalists and The Atlanta Junior League.

Kaufman has one daughter.

LIVING THE DREAMS OF OUR ANCESTORS
*Monica Kaufman to the Grand Marshal's Luncheon,
Mobile Mardi Gras Association (Excerpts)*
Mobile, Alabama — February, 1998

We are a long, long way from our ancestral home, but in this month, we try to get in touch with our past as African Americans.

Today, you will learn facts and hear the thoughts of black people, but the message during this month is for all people.

Let us begin with a proverb from the continent of Africa. In Ethiopia they say, "He, who learns, teaches." What you learn today, about black history in America, pass on to others: Each one, teach one.

And that appears to have been the premise for Dr. Carter G. Woodson, the father of black history, when he founded the association for the study of Negro life and history.

He began with Negro History Week in 1926. That week purposely included the birthdays of President Abraham Lincoln on Feb. 12 (he freed the slaves with the Emancipation Proclamation) and the Feb. 14 birthday of the great black abolitionist and orator, Frederick Douglass.

Woodson wrote in 1926, "If a race has no recorded history, its achievements would be forgotten and in time, claimed by other groups. The achievements of the Negro properly set forth will crown him as a factor in early human progress and a maker of modern civilization.

"He has supplied the demand for labor of a large area of our country. He has given the nation a poetic stimulus. He has developed the most popular music of the modern era. In his native country, moreover, he produced in the ancient world, a civilization contemporaneous with that of the nations of the early Mediterranean. He influenced the cultures then cast in the crucible of time. Must we let this generation continue ignorant of these eloquent facts?"

A question asked in 1926 is still relevant in 1998.

And the answer is the same: No, because there are lessons to be learned from those who made black history.

What Woodson said is true: Our achievements have been forgotten and claimed by others.

Let's just look at a few. Thomas Edison is called the inventor of the light bulb. But he was the co-inventor. Lewis Latimer was the other co-inventor. He was the only black member of the Edison pioneers. He invented the carbon filament for the electric light bulb and the bulb's threaded socket.

Our children learn Eli Whitney invented the cotton gin, but they are never told he was a black man.

The American Red Cross wouldn't exist if it hadn't been for Dr. Charles Drew, a black man who pioneered the process for storing blood plasma during World War II and created the first blood bank.

Open-heart surgery is routine now, but the first successful open-heart surgery was done by a black physician, Daniel Hale Williams, in 1893 in a Chicago hospital.

Madam C.J. Walker became the nation's first black woman millionaire by inventing the straightening comb and a skin whitener.

But it is in the field of agriculture where we see black Americans changing the money-making power for all Americans.

The poultry industry was revolutionized by a black man, Granville T. Woods. In 1890, he invented a new and improved egg incubator. It gave chicken farmers the ability to hatch 50,000 eggs at one time.

There is a connecting line between George Washington Carver and former President Jimmy Carter.

Carver was an agricultural scientist at Tuskegee Institute who found over 300 uses for the peanut. That made it a cash crop. The Carter family wealth is built on the peanut.

And then there is Benjamin Banneker, who used his mind to the fullest when we were thought not to have one. He was an astronomer, mathematician and surveyor, who helped design the city of Washington, D.C., at the age of 19. In 1723, he invented a striking clock from wood that kept perfect time for 40 years.

Banneker also was a man of letters. When then-Secretary of State Thomas Jefferson said that people of color were inferior to whites, Banneker wrote back that "the color of the skin is in no way connected with the strength of the mind or intellectual powers." What an eloquent statement, written by a man who wasn't considered by some people as even a human being.

This month is not just a time to catalogue all the firsts of black America, to educate people about what we've done. It is also a month to learn the lessons, taught by those who made our history.

The first lesson is what my mother always has preached: "It is what you do with what you have that makes you what you are."

It is committing yourself to being the best person you can be, looking within and realizing you have the power to be and do all that you want to be.

The people who made black history understood what the United Negro College Fund has long said: "A mind is a terrible thing to waste." They didn't make excuses; they made work. They didn't wait for changes to come; they made changes.

The lesson in black history is to use your mind to the fullest.

The next lesson from black history: If those who made history could succeed when the odds were against them, when they had no rights and were considered less than human, ignorant, property ... if they could succeed and make contributions and inventions that all people still use around the world, then this generation has no excuse for not being successful.

Those who lived our history made a way out of no way. They put up with it, so we could take advantage of it.

They were dreamers, and Poet Langston Hughes asked what happens to a dream deferred.

"What happens to a dream deferred? Does it dry up like a raisin in the sun? Or fester like a sore ... and then run? Does it stink like rotten meat? Or crust and sugar over, like syrupy sweet? Maybe it just sags like a heavy load. Or does it explode?"

We are living the dreams of our ancestors.

Their dreams exploded into reality, because they were a determined people.

Frederick Douglass wrote about the importance of self-determination:

"Our destiny is largely in our own hands. If we find, we shall have to seek. If we succeed in the race of life, it must be by our own energies and our own exertions. Others may clear the road, but we must go forward."

And that leads us to the third lesson from black history: Our ancestors were not afraid of hard work. To them, all work was good work, as long as it was honest work. We need all careers, and each is important. The president of the United States can be inconvenienced by a stopped-up commode that he can't fix. A plumber is needed.

Booker T. Washington wrote about the value of hard work and all occupations:

"Patiently, quietly, doggedly, persistently, through summer and winter, sunshine and shadow, by self-sacrifice, by foresight, by honesty and industry, we must reinforce argument with results."

He basically admonished us not just to 'talk the talk,' but to 'walk the walk,' to lead by example.

We need all careers, and each is important. The president of the United States can be inconvenienced by a stopped-up commode that he can't fix. A plumber is needed.

The next lesson taught by those who wrote our history: You must be a person of character.

The Josephson Institute of Ethics defines a person of character as a good person, someone to look up to and admire. A person of character knows the difference between right and wrong; always tries to do what is right; sets a good example for everyone; makes the world a better place; and lives according to the six pillars of character — trustworthiness, respect, responsibility, fairness, caring and citizenship.

The last lesson of black history: It is not just our history; it is everyone's history, because we all still benefit from it.

And the lessons taught by those who made black history — their values, what they did and how they did it — are not just messages applicable to black folk, but to all folk.

We all can learn from the lives of those who've passed on. So this month, recommit yourself to follow in the footsteps of those who came before. Learn from the past. Recommit yourself to live in the present, working to better our lives and the lives of others, to make our country, our cities, our neighborhoods, what they should be. And then, recommit yourself to prepare the next generation for the future.

And our theme songs should include more than "We Shall Overcome," but also:

> *Ain't gonna let nobody turn me round,*
> *turn me round, turn me round.*
> *Ain't gonna let nobody turn me round.*
> *Gonna keep on walking, keep on talking,*
> *climbing up to kingdom land.*

Patricia Russell-McCloud

Patricia Russell-McCloud is president of Russell-McCloud and Associates. She is a professional orator and author, making more than 100 speeches annually to corporations, government agencies, colleges and universities, and civic and community organizations around the world.

Russell-McCloud is immediate past president and a member of the board of directors of The Links Inc. and The Links Foundation Inc. She has also served on the boards of the Georgia Association of Minority Entrepreneurs and the National Black College Alumni Hall of Fame. She is a life member of the NAACP. *Black Enterprise* magazine has called her one of the top five business motivators in America.

Russell-McCloud's most recent book, *A is for Attitude: An Alphabet for Living,* uses the alphabet as a touchstone, inspiring readers to reach their highest potential.

BRIDGES, NOT BARRIERS

Patricia Russell-McCloud to the National Association of Black Meeting Planners (Excerpts)

Las Vegas, Nevada — November, 1999

*L*ife is going to be a challenge. There are going to be rough places and difficult situations. There are going to be major obstacles, hurdles and stumbling blocks. And you're going to be required to turn those stumbling blocks into stepping stones, obstacles into opportunities, and barriers into benchmarks. And you're going to have to be empowered to say that even though you've reached the end of your rope, you have to be able to tie a knot and hold on.

Hush, somebody is calling your name.

I want to look at collaborative partnering and building bridges for successful meetings — bridges, not barriers. Think about the bridge. Think about a bridge giving you access and egress. Think about the Golden Gate Bridge in San Francisco and the Oakland Bay Bridge. And think about the Cabin John Bridge in Maryland and the Memorial Bridge that gives you ingress into Virginia. And the Thomas Roosevelt Bridge. Think about New York's Brooklyn Bridge and the Chesapeake Bay Bridge Tunnel. And think about what happens when you get caught in the tunnel, and what it means to just sit and wait when you have difficulties.

We need bridges, not barriers. If you keep your eye on the ball, your shoulder to the wheel and your ear to the grindstone, I doubt that you will be able to work in that position.

So what shall we do with what we know? We know that empowerment has to be more than a buzz phrase. Empowerment means that you can be ready to operate with firsthand information, because knowledge is power. Information is a positive response to a negative threat. Empowerment is seriousness of purpose and plan. It's a ready-set-go posture. It declares that if you're not on the way, you're in the way. You have to move out of the way. We need bridges, not barriers. There has to be an appreciation of who you are and Whose you are.

Hush, somebody is calling your name.

You have to understand that appreciation is a three-legged pedestal.

> *If you keep your eye on the ball,*
> *your shoulder to the wheel and your ear to the*
> *grindstone, I doubt that you will be able to*
> *work in that position.*

It has triple As. You have to have acceptance, approval and appreciation of one to the other. Because when you focus upon what makes an organization, association or group work, it's easier to join than it is to belong. It's easier to recommend than it is to carry out. It's more desirable to complain than to act upon your complaints. It's easier to receive the appointment than it is to fulfill the responsibilities of the job. And it's now more important to rely upon the immediate methods of communication, fax mail and express mail and voice mail and Internet, than it is to meet the deadline, to be on time with the times.

We complain about organizational culture, but we don't do very much about it. Hush, somebody is calling your name.

You're the homies or posse or best friends or colleagues or associates, whether in charge by appointment or as Johnny Cochran said, by "anointment", by election or whether you are one who is or one who wants to be, whether you are seasoned or young. And you understand that I am using the word *seasoned* rather than older, because once you get past 40 it becomes seasoned.

Think about what you want to say and how, and think about what the best solution is. And remember that acts have consequences. Remember now that even the three Rs have changed. Don't you remember when it was reading, writing and arithmetic? Now that's stretched to respect, responsibility and rational thinking. You need conflict-resolution skills. You need to know how to cope with copping-out as a requirement. You need to know that your body language has a message, all those winks and blinks and hands on your hip and the elastic neck. The goals and the objective are to know that you don't want to defeat yourself before the battle begins. So what shall we do with what we know? We know that the issue is to be active rather than reactive. We have problem-solving teams and work teams, virtual teams, quality teams and management teams. But it's interesting that much could get done if we weren't concerned about who is going to get the credit.

Hush, somebody is calling your name.

Teamwork is not simple. Some people live for conflict, and others live to avoid it. Some people are emotional and expressive, and others are rational and reserved. Some people are extroverts, and some people are introverts. But you see, this is called diversity. And diversity is a competitive advantage, because one size does not fit all.

I was working at the Federal Communications Commission and I thought I was really in charge. I had been elevated and elevated and elevated, and now I am senior managing attorney, so I just knew that everybody was going to be thrilled. Then all of a sudden, my senior attorney came to me and said to me, "I'd rather work for a black than work for a female." And I said, "And which one did you think was going to change?"

A young waiter was working — and Sen. Bill Bradley tells this on himself — and the senator wanted butter with his bread. He kept saying, "Young man, I would like butter, I would like butter. Just bring me some butter." Five minutes passed, and then 10, 11 and 12. And the senator said,"Sir, I would like butter with my bread. Butter, please." And then five more minutes passed and then 10 more minutes and then the senator was very upset. He said, "You do not seem to know who I am." And the young waiter said, "And who are you?"

He said, "I'm a senator of the United States of America. I've traveled the globe. I am somebody. I have keys to the city. I'm a renowned athlete. You do not seem to know who I am."

And the young waiter looked at the senator and said, "Senator, you do not seem to know who I am."

And the senator said, "And who are you?"

The waiter said, "I'm the man with the butter."

So you see: Never assume. The good rule to follow is never assume. Think before you speak, because in English there are 45 variables, which combine to form a subset of nine vowels, three semi-vowels and 21 consonants, and four stretches, four pitchers and four junctures. Always get ready to prepare, prepare, prepare. People can hear you within earshot.

Bridges, not barriers. Confucius spoke of it and the Buddhists spoke of it. The *Holy Bible* speaks of it, in this adage: Do unto others as you would have them do unto you. It's not, "Do unto others and hope they don't get around to doing unto you."

We haven't distinguished ourselves with our willingness to be caring and honest. Success drives us. It's killing us because at every level of success, there's always one more rung. Just one more rung. Hush, the standard of anything goes when anything does go. Frederick Douglas said it this way: "In life, you may not get everything you work for, but you're going to work for everything you get."

> *Remember now that even the three Rs have changed. Don't you remember when it was reading, writing and arithmetic? Now that's stretched to respect, responsibility and rational thinking.*

Hush, somebody is calling your name.

Appreciate the difference that we bring to the table. Appreciate the dimensions of each offering, the cohesiveness of working together rather than pulling apart — because the call is for synergy, synergy, synergy. And synergy does not mean that one plus one equals two. One plus one, side by side, can equal 11 or more.

We look at the men's training style or administering style: They have objective control. Women have objective change. Men tend to issue orders, and women act as role models. Men want the bottom line. Women are more empowering; they want an opinion. They want to talk about it. Women are intuitive. Women have a sixth sense. Men understand team play. Men can arrive at 10 o'clock. They can debate vociferously at 11 o'clock, but at 12 o'clock, those same two men are having lunch together. Women, it might take a little longer. And so, meeting planners learn to swim when the bridge is closed. Learn that the "isms" are still here, the racism and the classism and the sexism. Learn to swim in shark-infested waters. All waters won't be welcoming in your industry. You're in a tough industry, hospitality. You have to learn to breathe and stroke. You may not have oxygen, but your responsibility is to hook up with somebody who has the oxygen. Learn to breathe and stroke, then tread water to stay afloat. Why? Because every 24 hours the whole world rotates over the person who thought he or she was sitting on top of it.

And then finally, when you're in shark-infested waters, just remember that you will not be able to identify everything in the water. Some will look like fish and they'll be sharks. Some will look like sharks, and they'll be fish. Some will be of your color and not of your kind. Some will be of your kind and not of your color. So build bridges, not barriers.

Cynthia A. McKinney

Cynthia A. McKinney represents the 4th Congressional District of Georgia as a member of the House of Representatives in the U.S. Congress. She was Georgia's first African-American congresswoman and is the only woman serving in the state's congressional delegation.

McKinney was appointed to the Armed Services Committee and is a member of the International Relations Committee, serving as ranking member on its International Operations and Human Rights Subcommittee. She was the House sponsor of the Arms Transfers Code of Conduct, which aims to prevent the sale of U.S. weapons to dictators.

McKinney is a member of the Congressional Black Caucus and the Progressive Caucus and works closely with the Hispanic Caucus. She has assisted a number of Georgia-based companies in establishing and strengthening trade relations with African nations.

McKinney has one son, Coy.

DO YOU SEE WHAT I SEE?

Cynthia A. McKinney to the MLK Jr. Commemoration Service,
Ebenezer Baptist Church

Atlanta — January, 2001

Just before Christmas, I took a walk in Washington along the route of presidential motorcades. What I saw was shocking. And made me think about the state of black America and the sacrifices that Dr. Martin Luther King, his family and his generation made for us today.

Let me tell you what I saw.

In the same block as the White House on that cold winter's night, I saw an elderly black woman wrapped in old newspapers, huddled in a bus shelter.

As I walked along Pennsylvania Avenue, I saw black man after black man after black man in makeshift cardboard beds, sleeping on sidewalk benches, over heating grates and under bridges. In the city's nooks and crannies, I saw black men, discarded like trash, on the streets of America.

On the streets of America, do you see what I see?

The Justice Department admits that blacks are more likely than whites to be pulled over by police, imprisoned and put to death. And though blacks and whites have about the same rate of drug use, blacks are more likely to be arrested than whites and are more likely to receive longer prison sentences.

Twenty-six black men, some probably innocent, were executed last year; we start 2001 by executing a retarded black woman.

In the justice system of America, do you see what I see?

Government studies on health disparities confirm that blacks are less likely to receive surgery, transplants and prescription drugs than whites. Physicians are less likely to prescribe appropriate treatment for blacks than for whites, and black scientists, physicians and institutions are shut out of the funding stream to prevent all this.

Can you believe it's true that a black baby boy born in Harlem today has less chance of reaching age 65 than a baby born in Bangladesh?

In the healthcare of America, do you see what I see?

I serve in Congress where the Black Caucus is shrinking. Yet, sections of the Voting Rights Act will soon expire, and quite frankly, after crippling court decisions, there's not much left of Affirmative Action to mend.

I ask myself, after so much sacrifice, why are we going backward?

In the FBI's own words, its counterintelligence program had as a goal "to expose, disrupt, misdirect, discredit or otherwise neutralize" the activities of black organizations and to prevent black "leaders from gaining respectability."

> *Can you believe it's true that a black baby boy born in Harlem today has less chance of reaching age 65 than a baby born in Bangladesh?*

Remember, Geronimo Pratt spent 27 years in prison for a crime he didn't commit. Too many others, including many white allies targeted like Geronimo, age in prison today.

And instead of real leaders, COINTELPRO offers us hand-picked "court priests," who are more loyal to the plan than to the people. Court priests who preach peace, when there is no peace.

COINTELPRO was the plan, and we are what we are today because it was meant to be.

Dr. King well knew the enormity of what he was challenging, and yet, he and his family stood tall in the face of great danger.

The *Bible* mentions a special group of warriors who carried neither sword nor weapon. They were men who were prepared to defeat the greatest foe with only their words and wisdom. These were the Men of Issachar. Dr. King was such a man, a man whose indomitable courage united black and white America.

Dr. King could see what America wasn't ready to see. Dr. King wanted America to be what America wasn't ready to be. Dr. King rejected the court priests of his day. And for this, Dr. King paid the ultimate price.

Each and every year, we remember Dr. King. But we should also rededicate ourselves to his struggle.

Now I ask you for the very last time:

Do you see what I see?

Thelma Wyatt Cummings Moore

Thelma Wyatt Cummings Moore serves as judge of the Superior Court of Fulton County, presiding over civil, domestic and felony criminal matters. From 1998 to 2000, she served as the first female chief judge of that court, which is Georgia's busiest trial court of general jurisdiction.

Moore spearheaded the creation of "Family Court," which resolves multiple family disputes, focusing on the needs of children. As chief judge, Moore also spearheaded a project to design the Comprehensive Justice Information System for Fulton County, and served as chair of the Justice System Executive Committee and the Alternative Dispute Resolution Board.

Moore serves on the board of trustees of Emory University and is a former board member of the National Center for State Courts. She has received awards from numerous organizations, including the National Bar Association Judicial Council, the Atlanta Branch of the NAACP and Emory School of Law.

THE ROAD TO JUSTICE:
THE AFRICAN-AMERICAN LAWYER IN THE FOREFRONT

Thelma Wyatt Cummings Moore to the Auburn Avenue Research Library, Annie McPheeters Lecture (Excerpts)

Atlanta — April, 2000

I was born during the era of Jim Crow in a small town where our schools, water fountains, bathrooms, movie theaters and all public facilities were segregated. A $2 poll tax was imposed to deter African Americans from voting. My father, a medical doctor, was relegated to the basement of the hospital to treat his African-American and Hispanic patients. Early one morning in 1952, our house was burned down, we believed by the Klan.

Later, when the house was rebuilt, a cross was burned in the front yard and threats were made against us when my father had the audacity to run for the city school board. As a little girl, I had never heard of an African-American lawyer, let alone an African-American judge.

It was many years later that I learned about Charles Hamilton Houston, William Hastie, Thurgood Marshall, Constance Baker Motley, Donald Hollowell and, of course, Dr. Martin Luther King Jr. And I was inspired by my brother, J.O. Wyatt, to utilize the law as a tool for social change.

Just as I was inspired, I would like to share with you today on the subject of The Road to Justice: The African-American Lawyer in the Forefront.

For Atlantans, Auburn Avenue has been one road to equality. It is where African-American lawyers began the struggle for equal opportunity as they upheld our history, our culture and laid a foundation for a brighter future for African Americans.

Known for his gift of oratory and his brilliant leadership, A.T. Walden walked this very road. Walden is credited with increasing the number of African-American registered voters from 1,800 voters in 1910 to 25,000 in 1939.

After 25 years as a Georgia lawyer, Walden commented on the dearth of African-American lawyers in the South and was quoted in the *New York Times* in 1937. Citing racism in the law and tradition, Walden predicted that the future of African-American lawyers was "cloudy and even ominous."

In 1931, there were only five African-Americans lawyers in Atlanta and probably less than a dozen throughout the state. In 1941, the number of African-American lawyers dropped to seven. Only two African-American women were admitted to the Georgia Bar prior to 1944: Estella Henderson and Rachel Pruden Herndon.

In the face of struggle and adversity, the Gate City Bar Association was founded in 1948. African-American attorneys were denied admission to the voluntary bar associations, such as the Atlanta Bar Association, which limited membership to "white members of the bar in good standing and of good moral character."

Through the entity of the Gate City Bar Association, African-American lawyers were strengthened in their quest for civil rights, as well as in their professional and personal endeavors. They had been unable to attend continuing legal education seminars and disallowed from seeking the professional support of other members of the bar; thus, they founded and fostered their own organization.

A.T. Walden called together the 10 African-American attorneys who practiced in Atlanta to form the organization, and Walden was elected its first president. At the time, there were three groups of African-American attorneys practicing law in Atlanta: The Walden Group, comprised of A.T. Walden, Charles M. Clayton, E.D'Antignac and Rachel Pruden Herndon; the Henry Group, comprised of T.J. Henry, E.E. Moore Jr., S.S. Robinson and R.E. Thomas; and two independents, Col. J.E. Salter and Col. T.W. Holmes.

Another era for African Americans in the legal profession dawned in the Fifties when Donald Lee Hollowell, Romae Turner Powell and Isabel Gates Webster were admitted to the Georgia Bar. In fact, a great many of the civil rights cases, which resulted in the integration of public facilities, were argued by Gate City Bar Association members.

Of considerable note is the desegregation of the public university system in Georgia. For seven years, from 1950 to 1956, Horace Ward battled for admission to the University of Georgia Law School with the legal assistance of prominent civil rights attorneys Donald Hollowell, A.T. Walden, Constance Baker Motley and the full backing of Atlanta University Professor Dr. William Madison Boyd. The university was eventually desegregated when Hollowell and Ward, who by this time had earned his law degree at Northwestern University, succeeded in leading the fight for Charlayne Hunter Gault's and Hamilton Holmes' admission to the University of Georgia in 1961.

Isabel Gates Webster represented plaintiffs in the years-long effort to desegregate the city of Atlanta public schools and ran for a seat on the State Court of Fulton County. Romae Turner Powell became the first African American in modern times to sit on the bench of a state court of record when she was appointed judge of the Juvenile Court of Fulton County in 1973.

Undergirded by the valiant struggle of all who have gone before, the modern era has recorded more African Americans admitted to the bar then ever before.

About 80 African Americans now serve on benches in the courts of this state. African Americans are represented as corporate counsel, in governmental and non-profit agencies, in major law firms and as sole practitioners.

We must not rest on the soft cushion of complacency; rather, recognize complacency as a thorny stumbling block to progress.

Each step, from Walden and Herndon to Hollowell to Maynard Jackson to Robert Benham, Clarence Cooper and Leah Sears, each step along Auburn Avenue, each step on this road to justice, has brought us where we stand today, having crossed the threshold of the new millennium.

We stand solidly on the shoulders of those who had the tenacity, the courage and the commitment to stare injustice in the face and to valiantly build the bridges we have crossed into the 21st Century.

We continue to face obstacles that others have never been required to face, and yet, we emerge victorious, a tribute to our invincible courage, tenacity and strength. We must not rest on the soft cushion of complacency; rather, recognize complacency as a thorny stumbling block to progress.

Let our steps be bold and unfaltering in our determination to continue the journey begun so long ago to uphold our rights, our heritage and our culture. Let our voices continue to teach the next generation that when they log onto that microcomputer in the corporate suite, they must remember Aaron Bradley, who was wrongfully denied admission to the Georgia Bar. When they gain a seat on the New York Stock Exchange and manage billions in their portfolios and 401Ks, they must remember A.T. Walden. When they walk across the campuses at the University of Georgia or Georgia Tech or Georgia State or West Georgia, they must remember Donald Lee Hollowell and Horace Ward. When they are appointed to serve on the bench, they must remember Romae Turner Powell, Isabel Gates Webster and Clarence Cooper. When they garner that major contract, they must remember Mayor Maynard Jackson and send some of those capital gains to the APEX museum and to the United Negro College Fund. When they download from their CD-Roms onto their pocket computers and place them in Coach leather briefcases while wearing their Armani suits and St. John knits, they must remember.

> *Those who would preach must commune with the Source of all justice and mercy and remember all those who made their way by faith.*

They must remember those who could not even sit before the bar in the courtroom, those who could not join the bar associations, those who traveled the dangerous circuits to defend our civil rights and civil liberties. Through their remembrance, they must carry us further along the road to justice.

Those who would preach must commune with the Source of all justice and mercy and remember all those who made their way by faith.

We must continue to travel this road and build bridges even as we have entered the new millennium. African-American lawyers have trod in the forefront down this road to justice and equality to uphold our culture, our history, our heritage. Our journey down the long road to justice continues.

Brenda Joyce Muhammad

Brenda Joyce Muhammad is the founder of MOMS (Mothers of Murdered Sons and Daughters), an organization dedicated to stopping violence in America's communities.

Muhammad is also program director for the Victim-Witness Assistance Program, a component of the Metropolitan Atlanta Crime Commission. She represents the first educational district on the Atlanta Board of Education and served as the board's first African-American female president in 1998.

Muhammad serves on the board of six organizations and a major corporation, as well as serving on the advisory committees of three local and two national organizations.

BRENDA JOYCE MUHAMMAD

EMBRACING A NEW VISION IN THE 21ST CENTURY
Brenda J. Muhammad to the Butler Street YMCA's Hungry Club Forum
Atlanta — March, 2001

The women of Zeta Phi Beta have always been visionaries. Staunchly conscious and action-oriented, we have always seized the day, using the power of our sisterhood to impact changes that are expansive yet inclusive.

We are united by our mutual commitment to live our lives in service to God, our families and our communities. Our forward vision has shone through a foundation based on service, scholarship, sisterly love and the seven-point plan of community action. In all of our endeavors, we have embraced a new vision. But we do not stand alone. We stand on the shoulders of our beloved ancestors who made a way out of no way. Sisters who nursed a nation, both black and white, and still gave praise every day and in every way. It is their familiar majesty I would like to pay tribute to.

We come from women whose stars have shone through tragedy and triumph, who proudly wore the crown that was bestowed upon them by God himself. We carry on the legacy of those risk-takers, those *herstory-makers*. And our souls sit in wonder of how we got over.

Women like Soror Zora Neale Hurston, a pants-wearing, cigarette-smoking maverick who jumped over the sun. A brilliant scholar and woman who never took the easy way out knowing that when you've struck a woman, you've struck a rock. "I have stood on the peaky mountain wrapped in rainbows, with a harp and a sword in my hands," she once quipped.

We pay tribute to women like my beloved grandmother, Mallie Harris. An identical twin born in Greenville, S.C., to an enslaved African, she raised me up in the way she wanted me to go when my 15-year-old mother could not meet the challenge. She guided and molded me like subtle clay, knowing that I could be anything I wanted, if I believed. And I thank her with all my heart.

Women like my grandmother worked from *can't see* to *can't see* in service to the Lord and family. She, like those that came before her, made the mundane spiritual and the spiritual mundane. Each of us, sisters, are anchored by the strength and fortitude of women like these, whose vision and dreams penetrated and shattered notions of being three-fourths and second-class. Our grandmothers and great-grandmothers raised a nation, never ceasing to see the blessings in each new day and opportunity.

We have made some hard choices and been challenged by the courage it took to come through the fire to the other side. But we've never let adversity diminish our hopes for the future – we are always making things more beautiful than we found them.

I'd like to pay homage to the founding mothers of our illustrious organization. Their vision was larger than their personal circumstances. They embodied the power of sisterhood, often times, in the midst of adversity. Their visions for the 20th Century link our vision for this new time, a time that is ripe with unique and substantial challenges.

The challenge of black men and women infected with HIV and AIDS; the more than 1 million men and women languishing in prisons; homeless mothers and Vietnam veterans who are battling mental illness; children raising children; academic institutions where the brilliance of our youth is diminished and unrealized.

In a time of unheard-of opulence, we seemingly lack the mental and spiritual fortitude to find solutions for what ails our families and our communities. Though the challenge may seem severe, we must heal our nation. If not us, then who? But we cannot save our nation without the support and love of our husbands, fathers and sons. This requires that we first heal our relationships with our men. We must forgive them for not saving us from the ravages of slavery, for not overcoming the societal images that have separated us since our arrival here on these shores. We must use love as our weapon. Our children and communities await our meeting this challenge. And we must remember who we really are – women who are doers, forward-thinkers, healers.

We have maintained a foundation of political, civic and community action. Our commitment to education, community volunteerism, government and economic development, health and wellness, and drug- and substance-abuse prevention must be commitments that we take to heart.

We come from women whose stars have shone through tragedy and triumph, who proudly wore the crown that was bestowed upon them by God himself.

We must sound the alarm so that our voices will be heard and, if necessary, expand our focus to include uncharted initiatives. We must cast our vote at every election, using our intelligence and love of self to raise the standards of our communities and this country as a whole. We cannot look to the larger society to find solutions that meet our specific needs. We must be truth-tellers, not letting complacency blind us to the needs of those of less material means. We must not let our personal privilege deter us from making changes – those hard choices that may put our wealth and status at risk. We cannot forget from whence we came. We were raised to be better than the best.

It has been *herstory* to rise to the challenge and I believe we can do it again. Will you join me in charting the blueprint for the 21st Century? The challenge awaits!

Susan E. Neugent

Susan E. Neugent is the president and chief executive officer of Fernbank Museum of Natural History.

Neugent is a graduate of Leadership Atlanta, Leadership DeKalb and the Regional Leadership Institute. She serves on the board of the Olmstead Linear Parks Alliance, the Atlanta Business League, the Georgia Wilderness Institute, Research Atlanta and the Girl Scout Council of Northwest Georgia. She also serves on the board of visitors of the CDC Foundation, Grady Health Systems and Georgia State University's School of Law. She is a member of the Downtown Rotary Club and the Women's Forum of Georgia.

Neugent and her husband, Dennis, have lived in the City of Atlanta since 1977.

SUSAN E. NEUGENT

THE IMPORTANCE OF NATURAL HISTORY
Susan Neugent to the Southeastern Council of Foundations (Excerpts)
Atlanta — May, 2000

I bet if we asked everyone in this room to define natural history, we would get 50 different answers. We all know what it is, but it's not as easy as it seems to articulate a definition.

Natural history is about science. And, through science, telling the story of the world and the people who live in it. But it's not just about the scientific history of the world and its people. It's also about our scientific understanding of the present and future of the world and its people.

It's not about history we collect – we collect phenomena. We collect the objects in nature because they give rise to ideas about nature. We collect the objects of culture because they give rise to ideas about our culture.

Natural history is about how human beings look at the world and their role in it. It is about the impact of the environment on people and the impact of people on the environment.

Natural history for some people suggests a place of dead animals and dead cultures. Natural history is about the science of the environment and human culture – certainly not dead but perhaps the two greatest issues of our time – environmental diversity and cultural diversity, and our understanding of them and their symbiotic relationship.

One of the most important functions of natural history museums is to reconnect man to nature and man to man. These alone make natural history museums especially relevant.

Two of the top three natural history museums in the world are in the United States: the American Museum in New York and the Field Museum in Chicago; the third of the top three is the British Museum in London. There are thousands of natural history museums in the world and more than 500 in the United States, varying in size and focus.

Many of those 500, though, are quirky little buildings full of taxidermy and rocks-in-a-box, frozen in time. Those are the ones that give you the image of dead cultures and animals when you think about natural history museums.

But when you think about the Field and the American, you think of wonderful, exciting, huge, multifocused institutions with much to see and experience, changing and updating on a regular basis. Fernbank wants to be counted in their company.

So, as I talk about challenges and opportunities we face, my discussions with my counterparts at the American and Field suggest that their challenges are not much different than ours. One of our challenges is that many people feel the word "museum" is boring right out of the box – we lose them before we can give them our message. As a result, many of us have thought about changing our names. Like, just "The Field," "The American" and "The Fernbank," not "museum of natural history."

We feel enormous pressure to have blockbuster exhibitions. These diminish really good, if not wildly popular, programming, but on the other hand, they keep you responsive to the market and, therefore, financially sound.

Another challenge — technology: Incorporating it, financing it, and replacing it on a regular basis to keep up with change. I believe that technology drives people to see the IMAX films as much as the subject matter. It is a whole new expense in the museum business, but it is essential to our future to connect with the 20-somethings and under. It's also part of reversing the boring image.

A third challenge — marketing: How do you get your message out unless you spend money on marketing? And marketing is no small expense. Even a million dollars won't get you much in a market the size of Atlanta, Chicago or New York.

Fernbank has a living collection that is the envy of the entire industry. It is the only museum in the world to have grown out of a natural area, much less a primeval forest. Fernbank Forest is 67 acres of old-growth Piedmont forest – the largest such assemblage remaining in the United States – and is among the largest urban forests in the world. It is a tremendous legacy. As a natural history museum that grew out of a primeval forest, we have a unique opportunity and an obligation to contribute toward the public discourse of these issues.

And what about Fernbank today? Fernbank is in its 29th month of economic recovery and growth. We have doubled our budget and made substantial additions to our technology and our facility. Attendance for the past two years has increased by 90 percent over previous years. And museum revenue attendance exceeds IMAX attendance for the first time ever.

What you may not know is that we teach more than 1,000 science classes at the museum every year, many of them involving the use of our scanning electron microscope – the only public SEM in Atlanta. We are very proud that our largest school group increase is in booking those classes. We have great potential to use the SEM for distance learning through the Internet.

Landing the Egyptian exhibition was a huge feather in our cap. It is recognized as one of the top two or three collections in the world. It is not a traveling exhibition in the traditional sense.

Securing the largest dinosaurs ever discovered for a permanent centerpiece for the museum is a great achievement. They are the Giganotosaurus – at 47 feet and 10 tons, the largest meat-eater ever discovered – bigger than T-rex; and the Argentinosaurus, at 120 feet and 100 tons, the largest plant-eater ever discovered. Fernbank will be the only museum (or any entity, for that matter) ever to mount the Argentinosaurus; and while the Giganotosaurus has been mounted a few times, Fernbank will be the only museum in the world to mount it together with the Argentinosaurus in the most dynamic scene ever attempted anywhere

Egypt, the dinosaurs and the other programming we do are part of a larger strategy to launch Fernbank onto the world stage with the top natural history museums, and someday, surpass them.

Fernbank is on the road to becoming one of the great natural history institutions in the world. We want people to cite our name along with the American and the Field as the very best. We want to be the "go to" entity on matters of the environment and human culture. Of course, that's what we do in Atlanta. We work to become No.1. And Fernbank will be no different.

Jenny Pruitt

Jenny Pruitt is president and chief executive officer of Jenny Pruitt and Associates, Realtors.

Pruitt is the president of the Atlanta Board of Realtors and is a member of the board of directors of the Georgia Association of Realtors, the Atlanta Chamber of Commerce, the Buckhead Coalition and the American Red Cross. In 1999, Pruitt was inducted into the Georgia State University Hall of Fame. She serves on the advisory council of Blue Print Sandy Springs and the Women's Resource Center to End Domestic Violence, and is a member of the Rotary Club of Atlanta and the Piedmont Auxiliary.

Pruitt's company has built two homes for Habitat for Humanity and is involved in providing Christmas gifts and contributions to children in inner-city Atlanta. In 1999, Pruitt received the Legacy Award from Big Brothers Big Sisters of Metro Atlanta for her contribution to the community.

EIGHT PRINCIPLES OF LEADERSHIP
Jenny Pruitt to the Sandy Springs Rotary Club (Excerpts)
Atlanta — September, 1999

Being involved in real estate in Atlanta has been very exciting. It's always a hot topic at cocktail parties and people are always interested in the factors that drive the market. Besides location, these factors are quality of life, the strength and number of neighborhood schools, the amount of protected green space, access to a major job market, and culture, services and recreation.

And there's good news about Atlanta. Our city will lead the United States in job creation for the next 25 years, resulting in 1.8 million new jobs. Atlanta has a terrific economic base with diversity in all sectors, including manufacturing, service, retail, education and government.

But there is also some not-so-good news. Hartsfield Airport is at capacity, and it will take at least 10 years to build a new airport. Alabama and Florida have filed lawsuits alleging that Atlanta is over-using the Chattahoochee River Basin, our main water supply. We are seeing more frequent smog alerts in our area, and newcomers are putting a great strain on our existing infrastructure. Atlanta has the longest average commute in the United States at 34 miles, and the lowest vehicle occupancy in the United States, 1.1 person per car.

There is good news and there is bad news, but I believe the long-term fundamentals are healthy and anyone who can establish a credit record can be a homeowner.

I feel so privileged and so blessed to have had the opportunity to be an entrepreneur and to have my own business in America and in this fair city of Atlanta. I am so proud to call Atlanta home.

Someone recently asked me to give them the characteristics of an effective leader. I thought about that question for a while and decided on eight principles of leadership that I subscribe to. I truly feel it is an attitude – what we call "Servant Leadership" in our company.

There is a saying that, "If you want to be a leader, you'll probably be disappointed because most people don't want to be led. But if you want to be a servant, you'll be fulfilled because everyone wants to be

> *It is inspirational leadership in a society hungry for leaders that will stand up against wrong and reach out to embrace what is right and good. It is like a light unto a dark world*

served." Our spouses, children, people we work with, and our friends all want to be served. These eight principles are:

1. Courage – Take a chance. Have the courage to stand up for your convictions.

2. Morality – Knowing what is right and sticking to your beliefs. Making the right choices and being able to say, "This is nonsense," when something is wrong. People want to look at their leaders and feel that they are someone to model their life after, to be a good example.

3. An Encourager – Give hope to someone you know or work with. Everyone needs a pat on the back and the words, "job well done." Be an inspiration for those around you.

4. Values – Your value system is the cornerstone of real success.

5. Ethics – Your reputation will follow you. People can influence 16 other people for good or for bad. Make sure what you relay to others is good because you are building your business on communication.

6. Integrity – People have to be able to trust you and know that you will be the same in private as you are in public. Trust is the hardest thing to get and the easiest thing to lose.

7. Modeling – Someone is always watching. You must stay the course, stay focused and stand in the gap for your people. Be a model for those around you as to how we handle stress, anger and failure.

8. Openness – Transparency – Communicate past mistakes. True strength is expressed in vulnerability. There are few things you can do that will build more loyalty and respect than confessing mistakes, asking for forgiveness when these mistakes hurt others, and being forthright and honest about every single problem that exists. Few people turn their faces from a humble servant leader who says, "Hey, I really messed up."

It is inspirational leadership in a society hungry for leaders that will stand up against wrong and reach out to embrace what is right and good. It is like a light unto a dark world.

Catherine L. Ross

Dr. Catherine L. Ross is the executive director of the Georgia Regional Transportation Authority (GRTA), which was created by Governor Roy Barnes to combat air pollution, traffic congestion and runaway development.

Ross serves on the national advisory board of the Women's Transportation Seminar and the Eno Transportation Foundation. She is a member of the board of directors for the Metropolitan Atlanta Rapid Transit Authority (MARTA) and the American Red Cross. She is also a member of the board of visitors for Emory University.

Ross was recently appointed to the executive committee of the Transportation Research Board, which reports to the National Research Council of the National Academies.

Ross lives in northwest Atlanta with her husband, Georgia Tech professor Dr. Thomas Boston. They have two children.

CATHERINE L. ROSS

EVERYBODY WANTS TO GO TO HEAVEN, BUT NOBODY WANTS TO DIE
Catherine L. Ross to the Regional Leadership Institute (Excerpts)
Atlanta — September, 2000

I want to talk about the importance of leadership and the role it must play in solving the problems that the Georgia Regional Transportation Authority was created to address.

Let me begin by telling you a bit about myself. I was raised in Cleveland, Ohio, and I attended Kent State University during the late 1960s. As you know, that was a turbulent time on America's college campuses and especially at Kent State. I will never forget the sorrow, fear and anger on our campus the day four students were killed.

At that point in my life, I didn't put much stock in the notion of leadership. I was convinced that there was something fundamentally wrong with our system, and that nothing an individual could do would make a significant difference. I spent a great deal of time studying systems, especially ones that were different from ours.

Today, I have come full circle, and I realize that not only does leadership matter, it is critical. One person can make a difference and cause change, both through the things she does, and perhaps most importantly, in the things she inspires and persuades others to do. It makes a difference who is included, who is in the room and who is at the table.

Today, as residents of the Atlanta region, we all have many things in common. We live in an area with a wonderful climate and plenty of natural beauty, from the Chattahoochee River to Sweetwater Creek to Stone Mountain Park. We have access to big-city amenities such as major league sports and museums, but many of us live in neighborhoods that retain a small-town feeling that folks in other big cities can only dream of. Finally, we all benefit from a regional economy that has been for several decades now, and continues to be, the envy of the Southeast, and in fact, the envy of most of the nation.

Unfortunately, we have one other thing in common: The quality of life that we all love so much is under attack on several fronts. Traffic congestion, poor air quality, a loss of green space and pollution of our rivers, streams and lakes are threatening our quality of life, and if that declines, our economy will surely follow.

I hope we will recognize our common interests and join together in a common effort to protect our quality of life. If we do that, if we pull together as Atlantans have always done at critical times in our city's history, I believe we have a chance to become a national model of how to address the unintended consequences of rapid growth. But it will require leadership, and that is where all of you come in.

Some of you might have heard an old blues song that includes the line, "Everybody wants to go to heaven, but nobody wants to die." That's how it is with some folks and transportation.

Everybody wants to drive on a brand-new open highway, but nobody wants it to cut through their neighborhood. Some folks say they would like to ride a train to work, but they don't want the kind of development close to their home that would be necessary to justify the expense of building a rail line. We recognize the problems with the status quo, but too often, we're afraid to try anything different because it is unknown, because the course is uncharted. I believe the future will demand we follow that uncharted course!

The solution – of course – is leadership. I don't think being a leader necessarily means that you have all the answers. But it means that you help create an environment and a process in which people who do have good ideas can craft answers and solutions.

We need to find a way to discuss these difficult, complex problems without becoming defensive or resorting to stereotypes.

Many of you are probably familiar with a report on sprawl in the Atlanta region that was issued early this year by Brookings Institution. That report reached some conclusions that are hardly news to any of us. For one thing, it pointed out that there is a great disparity in growth within our region. The northern suburbs continue to grow while areas on the southside can't even get a decent grocery store.

Secondly, the report showed how problems on the northside, such as too much traffic, are connected to the problems of the southside, like not enough development. This is food for thought, because it underscores the basic point that many of our problems are related. We already know that we can't solve our traffic woes without also looking at land-use patterns. But this report also shows that housing and schools are part of the equation. For example, there is a lack of affordable housing on the northside where most of the jobs are, forcing workers to drive long distances to their jobs, which creates traffic jams. Somehow, we have to find a way to give people more choices, so they won't have to drive if they don't want to.

Finally, the report concluded that Atlanta has a great opportunity to address these problems. If we succeed, we could become a laboratory for all the other cities in similar circumstances. We not only have an opportunity to protect our own quality of life for ourselves and our children; we can help people around the country who are grappling with the same problems.

This presents a wonderful opportunity, but it won't be easy. It will require leadership, commitment and resources. There is plenty of work to be done. If you want to lead, just pick a problem, roll up your sleeves and get to work. It might not seem like anybody is with you, but the road to solutions is often a lonely one.

Finally, I would sound a note of caution. It's easy for leaders to sometimes develop a too-elevated opinion of themselves and forget what is really important.

During his reign as heavyweight champion, Muhammad Ali was sitting in the first-class section of an airliner waiting for takeoff when a flight attendant asked him to buckle his seat belt.

Ali looked her right in the eye and said, "Superman don't need a seat belt."

The flight attendant, quite unruffled, looked right back and said, "Superman don't need an airplane, either."

That's what all leaders need – someone who can bring them gently back to earth when they get too carried away with themselves and their accomplishments.

Shelley Serdahely

Shelley Serdahely is president of the board of the Women's Resource Center to End Domestic Violence.

Serdahely's work with WRC is a continuation of more than 20 years of volunteering for and working in agencies whose mission is to end violence against women. She is also the executive director of the Jeanette Rankin Foundation, a national foundation that gives grants to low-income, mature women enrolled in college or a vocational training program.

SURVIVING DOMESTIC VIOLENCE

*Shelley Serdahely to the Women's Resource Center
Annual Luncheon (Excerpts)*

Atlanta — April, 2000

My job here today is to put a face on the statistics and stories you hear about domestic violence. I speak to you as a survivor of domestic abuse and as a woman who has spent years working to end violence against women.

This year I have heard, more than ever before, about women being violent and about men being victims. I honestly could not understand how people could think that women could batter men. Thinking of my own experience, being kicked in the back while shielding my infant son with my body because I had tried to escape, being forced to have sex while still bleeding from being punched in the face, having a gun held to my head while listening to complaints about my mother's interfering, I could not imagine how anyone could believe that women could be batterers.

Then I began to listen more carefully to what people were saying and began to understand how people could think that. There are relationships in which conflict gets out of hand. Anger takes over. Frustration takes over. People slap, shove or punch each other. Maybe the woman does it – maybe the man does it – maybe they both do it. I began to realize that people think this is the same kind of abuse that causes women to come to the Women's Resource Center. Maybe in a few cases, it is. But mostly, it is not.

For the most part, women don't show up at the WRC fleeing from out-of-control anger. They are running from someone trying to control them with emotional and physical abuse. I recently read an article by a researcher, Michel Johnson, that helped me understand the difference. He describes the violence perpetrated on battered women: "Escalation in such cases may be prompted by either of two dynamics. First, if his partner resists his control, he may escalate the level of violence until she is subdued. Second, even if she submits, he may need to display that control, so no amount of compliance can assure a wife that she will not be beaten. For a woman to simply live her daily life, she is always in a position in which almost anything she does may be deemed a violation of her duties or a challenge to her partner's authority and thus defined as the cause of the violence she continues to experience."

I am beginning to understand that to give you a clearer picture of what it is like to be a battered woman, you need to hear less about the violent episodes. You have heard the horror stories. You have heard that over 50 women died last year in the state of Georgia at the hands of an intimate partner or ex-partner. You have heard about more women being injured by a loved one than by car accidents. All that tells you about is the violence itself, not what it is like to be battered.

What we have not told you is the day-to-day mundane story of what it is really like. Not the violence, but the grinding down of spirit and life. So, here I go.

I met Eddy when I was 19. I loved him. I remember sitting in the sunshine one morning writing a poem in which I called him my *forever man*. Just to be clear, I did not come from a violent home. My father would never have hit my mother. I was spanked once that I can remember. I did not confuse violence with love. I did, however, believe that it was my job to make my forever man happy.

He told me what I needed to do to make him happy. I needed to dress a certain way. I needed to talk a certain way. There were people I could speak to and people that I could not speak to. He chose the job I took. He dropped me off and picked me up from work. It made him happy for me to give him my paycheck. I was not allowed to go places without his approval. The rules changed sometimes, without my knowing it. I remember one incident when he slapped me for answering the telephone wrong. The next time it rang, I was afraid to answer, and he slapped me for making him answer the telephone.

Almost anything I did could be deemed a violation of his authority. And, if that happened, I would be pulled back into line with violence, the threat of violence or the threat that he would kill himself.

Every minute of every day I knew that I was in danger. Every minute of every day I was thinking about what made Eddy happy and what might make him hurt me. And when I tried to leave, I found out what most women who are not able to go to a shelter find out – leaving is much more dangerous than staying. He will stalk you, hunt you down and drag you back or kill you because leaving is the worst form of disobedience.

So, you see, these are not relationships in which conflict erupts into physical attack. What we are dealing with is the use of violence by men to control women. It is well thought out, even calculated. It is combined with other forms of control, like financial control, control of friendships and family connections, control of where she works and what kind of access she has to the rest of the world.

Every minute, that control was there. Every minute of every day I did everything I could to keep my forever man happy – the way he told me to do it. Until, like the women who come to the Women's Resource Center, I was able to get away without being killed. Now, I am a survivor. I actually call myself a thriver, because the gift that he gave me was the passion I have about ending violence against women. He gave me a powerful determination that no one should be forced to live in fear. That is the gift that I am giving to all of you.

Today, I stand before you as a fighter, a defender of women and children. I may not have recovered my full, loud voice, yet. I may still get scared when men talk loud or sound angry, but I am not that woman who sat on the steps and waited meekly to die. And how did I change from a battered woman to a champion of women? I was helped every step of the way. I was never alone. I was always surrounded by other women like Jean Douglas. I had teachers like Johnnetta Cole. I was supported by thousands of people like you. They did not know my name or my story, but they were there with me. Like you, they were prepared to take a stand to end violence against women. They said, "You don't have to live like that anymore if you choose not to." I chose not to, and they helped me.

You have all helped me without even knowing me. I thank you with my whole heart for my life and for the lives of the hundreds of other women you will help. Money is critical as you know. But what is more critical is that those women know that you are here for them. What is critical is that you refuse to tolerate violence against women in this community. Please continue to be there for them and for yourselves.

Debbie Shelton

Debbie Shelton has been active with many civic and cultural organizations. She was the director of youth programs for the Alliance Theatre Company/Atlanta Children's Theatre and program manager for venue staffing for the 1996 Centennial Olympic Games.

Shelton serves as the chair of the board of directors of the Alliance Theatre Company and is the secretary of the board of directors of the YWCA of Greater Atlanta. She is a member of the board of directors of the Starlight Children's Foundation, the Visiting Nurse Health System and the Alliance Française d'Atlanta.

Shelton and her husband, Charlie, have two daughters, Lara and Ashley, and two grandchildren.

MUSINGS ON THE ARTS

Debbie Shelton to the Alliance Theatre Company Board of Directors

Atlanta — January, 2001

When we were children, we played with our toys and created with them an imaginary world. We listened to adult relatives tell us stories about our families. We colored, either in coloring books or on sheets of paper with pencils, pens and — if someone wonderful had given them to us — the extra large box of Crayola crayons with all the colors. We listened to bedtime stories, had songs sung to us and played on simple musical instruments. We didn't know it, but we were creating art.

The arts are as essential a part of human development as the ability to stand upright and use an opposable thumb. From the very earliest days of our growth as a species, we've used the arts to explain the unknown and to represent the natural world. In the world of the Greeks and Romans, the arts were used to explain the relationship of the gods to human beings. In the early Christian world, the church used dance, drama, music, painting, sculpture and stained glass to tell the story of Christ and His relationship to humankind. No matter what the religion, the arts have been an essential part of transmitting a sacred message.

The arts traditionally define a culture and a time. It is impossible to think of Renaissance Italy without focusing on the explosion of art that occurred in Florence, Venice and Rome. Elizabethan England is linked inextricably to theatre and the works of Shakespeare and Marlowe. The Benin culture of Africa is known through its sculpture. When archeologists uncover an unknown tomb, it is the remnants of art that fascinate and tell us how people of that time lived and thought.

From the very earliest times, the arts have told basic stories. The relationship of God to humankind. How we appear to each other. Love. Death. Hatred. Fear. Each culture has its own tales which are intertwined with basic emotions, but tell these stories in a way which reflects how people of a given culture live and interact with each other. The arts have traditionally assisted people of a specific culture to understand their own past, to deal with the present and to dimly comprehend what will be the future. The arts tell us all how to understand each other and how to live together.

Until recently, the arts have been considered to be a critical part of the life of an individual, as well as to the life and soul of a city and of a nation. In many countries other than the United States, the arts hold a central place in the lives of the citizens of these countries, and these nations underscore this belief by support of the arts and the institutions that produce the work. Unfortunately, such is not the case in our country and certainly not in our city.

> *The arts reach out to everyone in the community, providing a catalyst for audiences of all ages, races and colors to meet on common ground to hear common stories.*

Studies indicate that participation in the arts is an economic engine for a city and a motivator for students. In Atlanta, the arts generate over $700 million annually in economic impact and are the 7th largest non-governmental employer in the metro Atlanta area. These studies also indicate that the presence of a vital and vibrant arts scene attracts professionals to a city and is a factor in the retention of high-quality employees. Student interest in academic disciplines is enhanced by participation in the arts. The arts encourage volunteerism, and indeed, would not survive without volunteers. The arts reach out to everyone in the community, providing a catalyst for audiences of all ages, races and colors to meet on common ground to hear common stories. By so doing, the arts can help change attitudes and break down barriers, stereotypes and prejudices.

Atlanta has stated proudly for many years that it is a leader in the arts throughout the South. Certainly, the excellence of the work that is produced is second to none. However, Atlanta is not a leader in support of the arts and, indeed, lags behind its sister cities in the region. To quote the Research Atlanta study published in December 2000, "of the nine Southern cities studied ... Atlanta is in the bottom tier of Southern cities in nonprofit arts revenues per capita, philanthropy to the arts per capita and number of arts nonprofit per capita." If we are to continue to reap the benefits that the arts provide, we must support the work.

Artists who live and work in our community send their children to school with ours. They live down the street and worship in the same places that we do. They pay taxes and worry about the same urban issues that concern us all. They fuel the economic engine that has been the metro Atlanta area.

At the same time, these men and women are creating a mirror for us. Through their stories, they reflect who we were, who we are and who we may become. If we are to understand each other and learn how to live with one another, it is critical that we pay attention to artists and the work they produce. It is important that we participate in the arts and encourage our children to do the same — not only for the tangible benefits in learning that will result, but for the intangible benefits that derive from a common understanding of our own and others' stories.

Art can change lives.

Alana Smith Shepherd

Alana Smith Shepherd is a founding board member of Shepherd Center, the largest private, not-for-profit hospital in the United States providing care for people with spinal cord injuries, acquired brain injuries, multiple sclerosis and other neurological disorders, and urological problems.

Shepherd received the *Atlanta Business Chronicle's* Healthcare Heroes Lifetime Achievement Award in 2000. She is a member of the board of Atlanta Medical Heritage and the Buckhead Coalition and serves as an advisory director for the Spina Bifida Association. She is also on the advisory board of the George West Mental Health Foundation.

Shepherd is married to Harold Shepherd, owner of Shepherd Construction Company. They have three grown children, James, Dana and Thomas.

A MEANINGFUL LIFE

Alana Shepherd to the Westminister School Graduation

Atlanta — May, 1998

ongratulations to all of you upon achieving a distinction that will work for you forever — a Westminster education.

There was a time when commencement speeches were supposed to be lofty and long. Hopefully, this won't be either. I'll take just a few minutes to encourage you in three very practical ways.

You won't need to wait until you are 30- or 40-years-old to use these messages — although they will still work then, too. But what I say today will apply in your life tomorrow, next fall at college, anytime.

First, if you want to enrich yourself, *give* yourself. Volunteer. Make volunteering an integral part of your life, like working, sleeping and breathing.

Often we hear people speak of volunteering in terms of "giving back," and truly all of us do have that obligation to our community. But what I hope you will understand is that first and foremost, through volunteering, you give *to* yourself. The excitement of new people, ideas and challenges, and the joy of knowing that something good and significant has taken shape in part through your efforts, only enhance your personal growth.

If this class is like society as a whole, there are some of you who've done a lot, and many others who've always meant to do more than you do. It's time to turn those good intentions into action and to make volunteering a lifelong practice.

Perhaps you're not sure where you want to commit your time and energy. Don't let that stop you. Just follow your interests and convictions.

Even at your young age, you won't lack opportunities. Many colleges these days encourage their students to get involved in the community, especially with local schools and children. You'll find campus organizations that offer interesting volunteer opportunities. Or you might turn to religious institutions, Boys and Girls Clubs, children's shelters or any number of other worthy groups that couldn't open their doors and turn on the lights without the devotion of volunteers.

But how do you get started, you might ask? When somebody asks, "Who will do this?" just put your hand up. There's no worthwhile task that's beneath any of us, whether it's stuffing envelopes or making Kool-Aid for the tee-ball team.

Don't wait to be a parent to help coach soccer or work with a tennis clinic or keep score for church league basketball. Do that now.

At the same time, know how capable you really are. When you get involved with a nonprofit, you can be sure that leadership opportunities will come your way. Step up to the ones that match your skills and that give you a chance to grow new skills.

Organize the fund-raiser. Rewrite the by-laws. Run the membership campaign. Serve on the board – not just as a name on the letterhead, but as a working, doing director.

If you ever hear yourself saying, "Sorry, I'm just too busy," stop and take stock. How we use time is nothing less than a mirror of our deepest and dearest priorities. And that's a mirror we all need to look at on a regular basis.

My second message might sound at first as if it's mainly for the female members of the class, but it's really for everybody.

To the young women: I urge you to take charge of your own destiny. Whether you pursue a career, concentrate on a family or attempt to do both, be in command of your own affairs. Be prepared to support yourself. If Prince Charming comes along, fine; but you are responsible for yourself.

Don't give in to glass ceilings, external expectations or other forces outside yourself. Be true to your own sense of what's right for you.

Forge ahead toward your own goals – not stridently, but with a gracious, determined competence that goes much farther than shrillness or belligerence ever will.

And to you young men, give a hand to your sisters and to your female friends and classmates in their ambition to reach the same level of achievement and contribution that you strive to make. It's the right thing to do.

Just remember, the more open and encouraging you are toward others, the more ability and talent you'll discover within your peers and within yourself as well.

If you are leaving Westminster as I left North Avenue Presbyterian School – not at the head of the class – you can still emerge as a leader in your own time and in your own way. Twenty years ago, not many people would have picked Bill Gates out of a crowd to become the next great pioneer of American business.

Every one of you has a contribution to make, regardless of GPA, SAT score, class distinctions or any other factor. All of us can make a meaningful and positive mark, as long as we're steadfast in pursuing our goal.

Which leads me to my third message. This, too, is a truth for all ages: Be kind and caring to each other, even when it's not easy or comfortable. In fact, especially when it's not easy or comfortable.

Let me be precise about what I mean. There are going to be times in your life when someone you know goes through a tragedy, maybe a death in the family, or a crippling accident or another desperate situation.

It seems awful; it is awful. You're pulled between the feeling that you ought to do something and the fear that you won't know what to say and might even make a fool of yourself. Don't stay away because you want to remember them as they were before this happened. Don't say, "I just can't handle this," or, "I'm not a good hospital visitor." What if you were the patient?

A soft touch on the cheek, and an "I stopped by to say hello" will do wonders.

Nobody expects you to come with pearls of wisdom; just bring your compassion. You don't have to stay for hours; just a few minutes will do. You don't have to come everyday; just often enough to keep in touch.

And when you've done something to touch a friend's life, you'll have the most amazing mix of feelings. You'll feel important and insignificant at the same time, even if you hardly said a word.

There is power in your presence; you have no idea how much.

In fact, you leave this school with more power than you can possibly imagine. You have the power to do good in so many ways.

I heard of a young African school girl from a very poor family who gave her teacher a beautiful sea shell as a gift.

The teacher was touched. She knew the shore was miles away and the young girl had gone a long distance to find the shell. As the teacher said thank you, she also added, "But you shouldn't have walked so far."

And the young girl replied, "Ah, but Teacher, the journey was part of the gift."

God bless each of you on your own journey. May it return many gifts to you as well as others.

Betty L. Siegel

Dr. Betty L. Siegel is the first woman to head an institution in the University System of Georgia and serves as president of Kennesaw State University.

Siegel is a member of the board of directors of the American Association of State Colleges and Universities and the American Council on Education. *Georgia Trend* magazine named her among the 100 Most Influential Georgians in 1990, 1992, 1998, 1999 and 2000. Siegel serves on many community service boards, including the Atlanta Ballet, Junior Achievement of Georgia and the Northside Hospital Foundation. She is a member of the Atlanta Kiwanis Club, the Georgia Executive Women's Network, and the National Advisory Panel of The Women's Museum: An Institute for the Future.

Siegel is married to Dr. Joel H. Siegel, an attorney and associate professor of English at Dalton College. They have two sons, David and Michael, and two grandsons.

INVITING SUCCESS

Betty Siegel to the Salt Lake Community College,
Fall Convocation Address (Excerpts)

Salt Lake City, Utah — September, 1994

I'm going to talk to you today about inviting success. And I don't want you to think of me as being presumptuous for telling you about success, but I teach a class every year at my college called "Inviting Success After College." We've been looking long and hard at definitions of success, and here is the one that we've developed at our college: "Success is living the life you want to lead."

So, using that as my guide today, I want to read this one statement that will put my remarks into perspective.

Mary Hood, a great Southern writer, was on our campus recently. I want to read you a little statement that she wrote on the difference between a Northerner and a Southerner:

"Suppose a man was walking across a field. To the question, 'Who is that?' a Southerner would reply: 'Wasn't his granddaddy the one whose dog and him got struck by lightning on the steel bridge? Mama's third cousin – died before my time – they found his railroad watch in that eight-pound catfish's stomach the next summer just above the dam. The way he married for that new blue Cadillac automobile, reckon that's how come he's walking like he has on Sunday shoes, if that's who it is, and for sure it is.'

"A Northerner would reply to the same question, 'That's Joe Smith.' A Southerner might think (but be much too polite to say aloud), "They didn't ask his name – they asked who he is!' "

Who are we?

Warren Benis says, "Leaders are those who enroll others in their vision."

To be successful, we must honor work. Mazlow, the great psychologist, says that "true creativity is work that goes some place joyfully."

I learned about joyful work when I was at Cumberland College. When I went away to that little college, I came under the influence of a grand old man, who taught me what work is about. He was an old, old man when I was in his class.

He became very, very ill toward the end of his life, so ill that he couldn't walk to class. President Boswell used to send over two strong athletes every morning to pick up that poor old ailing professor and carry him, pack saddle, across the campus, lecturing as he went. I love the image of that.

When I went back to homecoming years later, before Professor Evans died, President Boswell said, "You ought to go over and see your favorite professor. I'm sure he'd want to see you." I walked over to Professor Evans' house on campus and walked into his living room where he lay wasting in a hospital bed.

I said, "Professor Evans, I've come back to tell you that I'm a teacher, all because of you." He said, "Let me see if I taught you anything." He used to teach in an old-fashioned way by calling off a quote from a card in his hand, and you had to answer with the rest of the quote. He called off some quote from so long ago, and I couldn't remember it. And he started crying. He said, "You know, Betty Fay, nobody ever remembers a thing I said." And I died. I didn't want to disappoint him. I said, "Oh, Professor Evans, you really must forgive me. I really don't remember what you said. I'm so sorry. But you know, I remember what you were." And he squeezed my hand, and he said, "That ought to be enough. That ought to be enough for any teacher."

It's not making a living that matters.
It's making a life.

And so I must tell you that when I think in terms of work, whether you're going into banking, or the ministry, or medicine, singing or whatever, it's not making a living that matters. It's making a life. Be about work in which you make a life, with passion, enthusiasm, excitement, generativity and empowerment.

The second point is: Honor not only work, honor learning.

We must keep on learning. Two years ago, the oldest student at our college was 75-years-old. She graduated after going to our college for 25 years, taking one class at a time. I made her stand at commencement and I said, "Addie, what are you going to do now that you've graduated?" She yelled back, "I'm going to teach."

She was in my office six months ago and I said, "Addie Smith, what are you doing back in school?" And she said, "I'm going to graduate school. I figure I've got 15 more good years." That's style.

My husband is a beautiful example of lifelong learning. He was a professor all of his adult life until he became 50, and at 50, he decided he wanted to go to law school. He came to me and said, "Betty, I want to go to law school in that five-year program at Georgia State, but I'm worried about it. If I go to law school, in five years I'm going to be 55." I said, "Joel, if you go to law school or not, in five years you're going to be 55 so you might as well go to law school." He went on to law school and was the oldest one in his class to graduate: 55-years-old. We bought him a seersucker suit. We bought him a bow tie. He looked like Matlock. We sent him into law practice.

One of the things I would say to all of us: We need not be afraid of growth, not be afraid of change, but to embrace it. Someone said that each age is a dream that is dying or one that is coming to birth.

The third point is how you honor self – who you are, using who you are as a solution for tomorrow. My friend, Celestine Sibley, writes for the Atlanta paper. She wrote recently that she went to the circus when she was a little girl and saw an elephant tethered to a stake in the ground. And she thought, as a child would, that the stake must run all the way to China, or else how could it keep that elephant, that mountainous animal, so securely tethered. At the end of her visit to the circus, she came back to look at her friend, the elephant, and the gamekeeper reached down and picked up the stake – and the stake was no longer than a pencil. And then she made this wonderful observation: What keeps us bound is not the stake; it is the idea of the stake.

So, may I suggest to all of us that we need to pick up the stakes that are no longer than a pencil in our lives.

The fourth point: Honor your family. Neal Postman, the author of *The Disappearance of Childhood*, has said, "Children are the living

*We need not be afraid of growth,
not be afraid of change, but to embrace it.
Someone said that each age is a dream that is
dying or one that is coming to birth.*

messages you send to a time you will not see." What messages are we going to send with our children? How many of you have children? Raise your hands.

Wrong.

All of us have children.

You're either a psychological parent or a biological parent – or often both. All of us send messages to a time we will not see.

I must suggest to all that our family is more than our immediate family. Our family is not just the family into which we're born, but friends are the family we choose. We all need a sense of community. Community is not a place; it is what is taking place. Let us create among us all a society in which we not only honor work and achievement, not only honor learning and continuing to learn, not only picking up stakes that are no longer than a pencil, but giving something back. Someone has said, "Service is the rent you pay on the space you spend on this earth."

My message has been what I hope faculty everywhere would want to say to students on this kind of day. Honor work. Be about true creativity that goes forward joyfully. Honor learning, and keep on learning all through life. Honor self, and pick up stakes that keep you bound. The stakes are no longer than a pencil. And, finally, honor others and be of service in your odyssey.

There will be no "givens" in your odyssey – in your quest for meaningful work, lifelong learning, self-fulfillment and service to family and community. But perhaps these words of the poet will comfort you on your odyssey:

I do not wish you joy without a sorrow
Nor endless day without healing dark
Nor brilliant sun without a restless shadow
Nor tides that never turn against your bark.

I wish you faith and love and strength and wisdom,
Goods, gold enough to help each needy one.
I wish you songs, but also blessed silence,
And God's sweet peace when every day is done.

Thank you very much.

Cathy W. Spraetz

Cathy W. Spraetz is the executive director of The Partnership Against Domestic Violence, which provides counseling, education, prevention programs and emergency shelter for battered women.

Spraetz is a member of the Georgia Society of Association Executives and the Atlanta Women's Network. She also served on the Governor's Council on Developmental Disabilities.

Before working with The Partnership Against Domestic Violence, Spraetz was the executive director for disability-focused organizations, including United Cerebral Palsy of Macon and Middle Georgia and Parent to Parent of Georgia Inc.

A native Atlantan, Spraetz resides in Lilburn.

PERSEVERANCE

Cathy Spraetz to the Georgia Executive Women's Network (Excerpts)

Atlanta — August, 2002

"You gain strength, courage and confidence by every experience in which you really stop to look fear in the face. You are able to say to yourself, 'I have lived through this horror, I can take the next thing that comes along.' You must do the thing you cannot do."

Eleanor Roosevelt

One of the hardest things a woman who survives domestic violence has to face is the decision to leave her batterer. In fact, the statistics tell us she may leave seven to nine times before she finds the courage and strength to leave for good. The first thing she has to do in order to leave is to "look fear in the face." To leave is to possibly put herself in mortal danger. To leave is to risk losing everything she has, including her children and all of her material possessions. To leave is to lose companionship, no matter how controlling. To leave is to become impoverished. To leave is to "break up" the family. To leave is to rely on the help of strangers. To leave is, in her mind, to admit failure. To leave is to do the thing she thinks she cannot do.

What we must do as a caring community is support her in her efforts to leave. To care, we must help her plan so that she takes the necessary steps to ensure her safety and the safety of her children. To care, we must offer her sanctuary so that during this period in her life she doesn't have to worry about having a roof over her head or food in her stomach. To care, we must offer her emotional support and nonjudgmental advice about her next steps. To care, we must offer her a hand up and a way out of what might look like insurmountable obstacles. To care, we must help her do the things she thinks she cannot do.

I continue to be inspired by the women I meet who have had the courage to leave an abusive relationship. I'm always amazed and somehow comforted by their strength and am proud to be standing alongside them, feeling richer for knowing them. Their struggle is not all that different than the struggle of some incredible women who made an impact on me at an early age. These were women I did not know personally, but felt I knew by reading about them and learning about their efforts to make a way for themselves against all odds.

On my 10th birthday, my grandparents gave me a book that transformed my life. It was called *The Miracle Worker* and was the story of Annie Sullivan and Helen Keller and the struggle each of them faced to break Helen's world of silence. I read about them over and over again and was mesmerized by Annie's tenacity of spirit and Helen's stubborn nature that was born of her strong sense of self. Helen and Annie's story is clearly about courage and strength and the will to triumph over what most would perceive as insurmountable obstacles.

Their story is the very thing that convinced me to begin my own career in the disability community, first, as a direct service provider working with preschoolers who were deaf and blind as a result of the 1967 Rubella epidemic that left thousands of children with sensory loss and varying degrees of mental retardation. Later, I found that my own strength and interest was in the administration of the programs and agencies that provided support. And so I began, in 1982, by serving as an agency Executive Director.

My work in the disability field most assuredly prepared me for the work I now do in the domestic violence community. There are common traits and struggles that are shared by both groups. Both have taught me so much about myself and how I choose to live my own life. They inspire me to work toward the common good of all women who struggle to overcome terrible circumstances.

As Executive Director for the Partnership Against Domestic Violence, I see courage and strength every day. These ordinary women who are living extraordinary lives because of their circumstances are shining examples of Helen Keller's belief that, "Character cannot be developed in ease and quiet. Only through experience of trial and suffering can the soul be strengthened, ambition inspired, and success achieved."

When I think of courage, I think of one special woman I refer to as "T," who woke up in a hospital bed after her ex-husband beat her, cut her throat and left her to die. In spite of it all, she survived. She had incredible strength and courage to leave her home thousands of miles away in order to start a new life for herself. "T," whose own character was strengthened because of her suffering, is now attending college and aspires to become a professional counselor in hopes of helping women triumph over seemingly insurmountable odds.

I challenge you to reach out to these extraordinary women, whether they are domestic violence survivors or single-parent mothers of special needs children, to offer compassion and support, and to recognize their heroic efforts in everyday living. I guarantee you that they will inspire you and that you will be forever changed by their stories of strength and courage. As Barbara Deming says, "We learn best to listen to our own voices if we are listening at the same time to other women whose stories, for all our differences, turn out, if we listen well, to be our stories also."

Karen Elaine Webster

Karen Elaine Webster represents District 2, at large, for the Fulton County Board of Commissioners. She is also senior corporate vice president of BEERS Skanska Inc., the largest commercial construction company in the Southeast.

Webster is a graduate of Leadership America, Leadership Georgia, Leadership Atlanta and the Regional Leadership Institute. She was named one of the 100 Most Influential Atlantans by the *Atlanta Business Chronicle* from 1999 to 2001 and one of the 100 Most Influential Georgians by *Georgia Trend* in 2000.

Webster has served on numerous boards, including the Atlanta Women's Fund, the Atlanta-Fulton County Water Resources Commission, the YWCA and the Southern Institute for Business & Professional Ethics. She has been a member of the League of Women Voters since 1985 and has served as chair of the League's annual luncheon. Webster is also a founding member of Hands on Atlanta.

WHAT DOES LEADERSHIP MEAN TO YOU?

Karen Elaine Webster to the
Leadership Athens Graduation (Excerpts)

Athens, Georgia — April, 2000

Ben Sweetland once said, "Success is a journey, not a destination. It is the journey, not the final destination that makes you a success." The decisions that you make from this day forward will determine how much you will enjoy life; it will determine all of the wonderful things that you have to look forward to and what impact you will make in your community. You must decide what road to travel. Remember, success is a journey.

If you do not remember anything else I say tonight, let me give you some simple advice: There is no right or wrong definition of success; you must decide for yourself. Don't ever let anyone define it for you. Webster's defines success as "the degree or measure of succeeding and a favorable or desired outcome." Ok - what does that mean? If you have a goal and you are able to attain that goal, then you will be successful. The definition is not predefined for you; it is not specific because you have to define the terms.

I enjoy the community service that I perform by serving the citizens that I represent as a public servant. Yes, it is truly public service to hold a full-time job and work a minimum of 30 hours per week for the citizens of Fulton County. I would encourage you not to only think of yourself, but to think of others. Each day across the United States and around the world, countless people from all walks of life spend time in service to others. Volunteering can be a transforming experience that changes one's perspective on people, on community and defining one's purpose in life. Volunteering is the civic rent you must pay. Giving part of yourself is much more difficult than giving money.

I will tell you, though, that I have been enjoying my position as a Fulton County Commissioner more lately. My focus for my first years was fiscal, but I now have had the opportunity to make positive impacts in a variety of areas. Recently, with the help of my constituents, I implemented a program to put more trees in the community. We took 1 percent of the Capital Improvement Budget and allocated it toward putting trees in every district of Fulton County. Trees not only beautify the community but they mitigate the effects of water and air pollution. I am sure that everyone knows the problems that we face in the metropolitan area; we have all sat on I-85 and seen the smog alert signs. Now that the mood is a little calmer at Fulton County, I feel that I can concentrate on making things better and not just reacting. I spent almost my entire first year just working on ways to strengthen our budgeting process and fighting against unnecessary spending and other so-called sweetheart deals.

> *Even though it is hard to go against the norm, I pray for the strength to use my head and follow my heart and make the right decision. I believe in the power of prayer.*

I am known as the "swing vote" and believe me, these have been difficult shoes to fill. No matter which way I vote, I am either too black, acting white, acting like a Republican or not acting like a Democrat. There are seven of us on the commission — four Democrats, including me, and three Republicans. My colleagues often say to their constituents that they do not have enough support to make things happen, and when they say this, they are talking about me. Imagine if I only voted with the Democrats or my fellow African Americans or with the women? Even though it is hard to go against the norm, I pray for the strength to use my head and follow my heart and make the right decision. I believe in the power of prayer.

We are getting ready to see some big changes in politics in the Atlanta area. As a result of the census, district lines will be redrawn. Blacks are very concerned that their power base will be diluted because, as you may know, we have experienced tremendous growth in the northern portion of Fulton County. In addition, the mayor of the city of Atlanta's seat will be available during this next election. Regardless of who wins, we will definitely see some changes. As a result of so many changes and uncertainty on the horizon, a political think tank group was formed to try to deal with some of these issues.

It is important as a leader that you recognize what is needed in your community and what you would like to do. It is important that you focus on areas that interest you, so that you really attain the success and appreciation that you desire. You must be happy in order to achieve success. Although saving a rare bird might be of importance to your community, if you are not passionate about birds or animals, it is best to focus on something that reflects your values. At BEERS Construction, we just spent a full day determining how to get our executives involved in the community. You would be surprised that these guys are the best builders in town, but leave them at a cocktail party alone for two seconds and they tend to mingle amongst themselves and fail to understand the importance of networking. Find your passion. I have found mine.

I love life and I love people!

There is no right or wrong definition of success; you must decide for yourself.

I have found that most people who work fall into two categories. They either live to work or they work to live. Only you can decide if you will fit in any category or box. Whatever you do from this point on, you must believe in yourself. Remember, your success or failure will determine your journey. You have heard people say that you can do whatever you want to do and you can, but you must believe. My minister always tells us not to listen to the joy suckers. Do you know any of those folks — always trying to steal your joy? If I had listened to them, I would never have run for office because I was told that (1) a black could never win countywide, (2) a woman could not raise money and (3) a woman could not win countywide.

What will separate you from the average Joe Q. Citizen? Always remember that the key to separate yourself from Mr. & Mrs. Average is to do more than what is expected and you will be rewarded.

Success comes in many forms, and it means something different for everyone. Search for your dream. There is a dream to capture for everyone out there. No matter what you do, do it well and success will come naturally. Set goals for yourself; self-promotion should not be your only motivation.

Now it's the time for me to stop preaching to you. I would, however, like to share this poem with you. Whenever I read this poem, it reminds me that I must stick with my goals no matter how difficult things seem. This poem is called *Anyway,* and it was published anonymously.

People are unreasonable, illogical and self-centered.
Love them anyway!

If you do good, people will accuse you of selfish ulterior motives.
Do good anyway!

The good you do today will be forgotten tomorrow.
Do good anyway!

If you are successful, you will win false friends and true enemies.
Succeed anyway!

Honesty and frankness make you vulnerable.
Be honest and frank anyway!

People favor underdogs, but follow only top dogs.
Fight for some underdogs anyway!

What you spend years building may be destroyed overnight.
Build anyway!

People really need help, but may attack you if you help them.
Help people anyway!

Give the world the best you have and you will get kicked in the teeth.
Give the world the best you've got anyway!

I am honored to have had the opportunity to be with you today. I wish you all the best of luck with your journey, professional and personal. Thank you. Godspeed.

Alice T. Wiggins

Alice T. Wiggins is the assistant general manager for external affairs at the Metropolitan Atlanta Rapid Transit Authority (MARTA), overseeing the offices of government and community relations, marketing and customer relations.

Wiggins serves as the vice chair of the American Public Transportation Association's (APTA) marketing steering committee. She is also on APTA's reauthorization committee and was recently appointed to serve on the U.S. Department of Transportation's 511 National Transportation Initiative. She serves on the board of directors for the American Red Cross and *Women Looking Ahead* magazine.

Wiggins is also involved with the Conference Of Minority Transportation Officials, the National Coalition of 100 Black Women, Women In Transit, the National Association of Female Executives, the Atlanta Ad Club and the Atlanta Chapter of the American Marketing Association.

MARTA'S COMMITMENT TO THE COMMUNITY

Alice T. Wiggins to the International Travel Association (Excerpts)
Atlanta — Spring, 2001

Transportation is a key element in our lives. We utilize transportation in many ways in our lives from our first baby steps to when we learn how to ride our first bike. As adults, we use automobiles, planes, buses, trains and a whole host of mechanisms to move around. Throughout our lives, mobility is key to our existence. Public transit is another means for people to have greater mobility in their lives.

The Metropolitan Atlanta Rapid Transmit Authority, known as MARTA, is the ninth largest transit system in the country and the 21st largest employer in Atlanta with over 4,800 employees. The authority is very much involved in the fabric of the Atlanta community, and we pride ourselves on the dedication of the people who work at MARTA.

MARTA has over $4 billion in capital assets along with our operating budgets and bond monies each year, all to support the daily operation of 38 rail stations (47.6 route miles of track and 248 rail cars) and 154 bus routes (704 bus fleet), which make up MARTA's transportation system.

We have recently embarked upon a very successful partnership with another transportation provider, Delta Air Lines, becoming the only transit authority in the country to offer our rail passengers traveling to the airport a full-service airline ticket counter in a MARTA rail station.

The latest figures project our daily passenger trips at 570,000 (50.1 percent trips on the buses and 49.9 percent on the trains), which represents a 20 percent increase in ridership since 1996 and the Olympic Games.

MARTA began over 20 years ago with a mission to provide comprehensive quality public transportation service in a safe and cost-effective manner, and we remain true to this goal today. The management and staff at MARTA frequently ask the question, "What is quality transportation?" in an effort to improve on service. And to the question of what is quality public transportation, several answers can be given:

• Enhances the mobility of the residents of the Atlanta region.

Throughout our lives, mobility is key to our existence. Public transit is another means for people to have greater mobility in their lives.

- Provides the public with a true alternative to the automobile.
- Plays a major part of the solution to regional congestion and air-quality problems for citizens who live in this region.

MARTA was created by an act of the Georgia Legislature in March of 1965 with a defined purpose: to plan, build and operate a rapid transit system within the metropolitan Atlanta area of Fulton, DeKalb, Clayton, Cobb and Gwinnett counties and the City of Atlanta.

Shortly after the MARTA act was passed, the MARTA referendum was also passed. The referendum succeeded in Fulton, DeKalb, Clayton and Gwinnett counties, and the City of Atlanta but failed in Cobb County. That referendum was followed by a 1971 referendum on a 1 percent sales tax to fund the system, which succeeded in Fulton, DeKalb and the city of Atlanta, all of which helps to define MARTA's operational boundaries today.

MARTA's strategic plan guides the authority's operation and planning, both long- and short-term, thereby setting management priorities and business strategies. It is also the basis plan management uses as a blueprint for all MARTA operations. The plan guides all objectives from development of strategic goals and objectives (annual budgets) to performance plans for individual employees.

MARTA's current strategic initiatives are:
- Customer focus.
- Transit advocacy.
- Employee development.
- Continuous quality improvement.
- Business management.

MARTA is involved in several long-term initiatives that will enhance its operation for the future. They include a two-mile extension with two new rail stations, Sandy Springs and North Springs stations, which were completed and opened on Dec. 16, 2000, at a combined cost of $463 million. Sixty-five percent of the total cost to build the two new stations came from federal funding. The stations, located in north Fulton County, are equipped with 2,400 parking spaces at North Springs and 1,325 spaces at Sandy Springs, in hopes that both stations will help encourage more people to park their cars and utilize public transit. The ridership at both stations is estimated at 6,000 patrons a day.

On the rail side, MARTA is making a substantial investment in upgrading its cars with the purchase of 100 new rail cars at a cost of $200.25 million. The federal government will assist us in our efforts by providing funding for the purchase of 56 of the 100 cars.

MARTA's bus fleet is also being upgraded to include the purchase of new CNG buses in keeping with MARTA's commitment to eventually have a full CNG-fuel bus fleet. It's our way of helping to improve Atlanta's air quality, while being good corporate neighbors to the community we serve.

> *The MARTA system is indeed the core of what can become a tremendous regional system unlike any other in this country, allowing other transit interests to build upon our system and existing infrastructure.*

Perhaps one of our most innovative projects is called TOD, or Transit Oriented Development. In 1997, the Federal Transit Administration ruled that a transit authority could utilize excess properties to generate additional revenues. Soon after the ruling, MARTA management recognized the opportunity to allow unused MARTA property to be developed for mixed-use projects by developers, while promoting transit in communities where these projects were designed. The Lindbergh Center project, located directly across from

MARTA headquarters, is expected to generate $10 million in revenue for the authority by 2008. Other TOD sites include projects at MARTA's Lakewood station, Chamblee, Abernathy Park and Ride lot, Medical Center and Ashby Street stations. MARTA's implementation of TOD projects is a shining example of how businesses and communities can partner to improve the quality of life for their residents.

Atlanta has experienced tremendous growth over the past 30 years and has become the largest metropolitan area in the South, encompassing over 14 counties. This explosion in population has spurred a need for regional planning in all major areas, such as education, business and transportation, with MARTA poised as the central provider of transportation. As a result, MARTA has been working with other transit agencies in the region, such as Cobb County Transit, to develop a regional plan for transit. MARTA has other reciprocal agreements with Gwinnett County and is currently in negotiations with Clayton County for future bus service for that area. Georgia Regional Transportation Authority (GRTA) is also exploring a regional express system and the possibility of commuter rail in certain high-density areas, along with the development of community TMAs (Transit Management Association) to ease congestion in the Atlanta metropolitan area.

With such an excellent record of providing our customers with quality, affordable public transit for over 20 years, MARTA's future is filled with infinite opportunities to expand our current system to provide millions of other customers the same quality service. The MARTA system is indeed the core of what can become a tremendous regional system unlike any other in this country, allowing other transit interests to build upon our system and existing infrastructure. However, in order to achieve our goals for the future, our customers, businesses, government and the community must all work together in a spirit of cooperation – to help maintain the system we know today and to propel us to that higher level of performance for generations to come.

Now you know why we are so proud of our agency and its employees. We're in the business of caring about our customers and their mobility. Just think about how life would be in Atlanta without MARTA and you'll see why we say, "Take MARTA, it's smarta!"

Linda Wind

Linda Wind is president of Wind Enterprises® Inc., a corporation committed to the personal and professional development of business and executive women and career mothers. The organization's Possible Woman® leadership conferences have been featured in numerous publications, including the *Wall Street Journal*. Wind's career previously included positions with IBM, Sharp Electronics, Pitney Bowes, Panasonic and AirTouch.

Wind, past-president of the Atlanta Women's Network, is a founding member of the Atlanta Women's Alliance and is actively involved with the Georgia Commission on Women and the Georgia 100 Mentor Program. She serves on the boards of the Northside Foundation, *Women Looking Ahead* magazine and Older Women's League. Wind is a member of the Georgia Executive Women's Network, The International Alliance, ABWA, Atlanta Women in Business, the Board of Directors Network and NAWBO. She is a graduate of Leadership Corpus Christi and Leadership Atlanta.

BECOMING THE POSSIBLE WOMAN

Linda Wind to the American Association for Women CPAs
Atlanta — May, 2001

Becoming the Possible Woman is the process of exploring the feminine wisdom, spirit and potential within. It is about realizing who we are as women, and what we may yet become. It means claiming our full potential and defining our strengths, talents and desires. The Possible Woman is a new model being created as we go along. It is about leadership, nurturance, compassion and intuition. It is also inclusion, synergy and making a difference. It is about working in full partnership with our male counterparts to create a better world. I encourage you to find answers to the questions, "Who are you?" and "What could you be?" as you walk the path of your individual life journey.

Now allow me to touch on some very revealing statistics that may give you a different perspective on your life forever.

Since the 1970s, we have tripled the percentages of elected officials who are women. Women comprise one-half the work force and hold one-half of all managerial positions in America. Women own more than 9 million businesses in the U.S., generating over $3.6 trillion in sales and employing 27.5 million workers.

We had only 13 percent of the PhDs in America before 1970, and now the numbers are well over 45 percent. We earn the majority of associate, bachelor's and master's degrees, and according to the *New York Times*, we are on the verge of becoming a majority in all U.S. law schools.

Women purchase 81 percent of all products and services, and consumer spending by women is $3.7 trillion per year.

Women are making the decisions for families. Seventy-five percent of all household finances are being handled by women, as well as more than 53 percent of the investment decisions.

Women bring in half or more of the income in most U.S. households today.

Of the net increase of the work force between 1992 and 2005, 62 percent are projected to be women. And according to figures published by Conde Nast, women are projected to acquire over 85 percent of the $12 trillion growth of U.S. private wealth between 1995 and 2010.

Women have more money than ever before. Women earn $1 trillion annually and represent more than 40 percent of all wealthy Americans, and in the year 2010, are projected to control $1 trillion in assets.

The new force is truly the power of the purse.

Not bad, considering that only 100 years ago, women were denied the right to vote, along with the idiots, the insane and the imbeciles. All that changed in 1920, with the efforts of Susan B. Anthony and Elizabeth Cady Stanton and the scores of women suffragists before them to literally affect the course of history. And change history we did! And we continue to do it daily.

Truly, we have all learned that when the scales are weighted in favor of one gender, or one race or one privileged background in a democracy, no one is very well served.

Now let's fast-forward to more recent days. In the 1950s, women couldn't serve on juries. We couldn't get credit in our own name in many parts of the United States until the mid-1970s, and that turnaround was because of Sarah Weddington.

Sarah was an attorney in Austin, Texas, who decided to add a law office to her home and was told that she couldn't get credit unless her husband signed for her. Now mind you, Sarah could make law in the Texas Legislature, she could argue law in the Supreme Court (Roe vs. Wade), but she couldn't get credit in her own name. Well, this was not pleasing to Sarah. As a result of Sarah going to the Texas Legislature to change this outdated and unfair law, women can now get credit without having a father, an uncle or someone off the streets to sign for her.

At first glance, our progress seems painfully slow, but we have covered a lot of distance in less than one lifetime.

And what have we learned?

We have learned that, regardless of our politics or our professions, one issue that matters is economic equality. Whether you like it or not, we live in a society where money matters. It does make a difference. And it is up to us to make sure we are fiscally responsible and can make decisions without having to depend on a man for our livelihood.

Understand that I am not proposing that women take over the world, or that we move from a patriarchal to a matriarchal society. Rather, I propose that we learn to work together with our male counterparts in full partnership with them, supporting and nurturing their efforts, learning from them as well as teaching, and complimenting their strengths in changing the world we live in.

Truly, we have all learned that when the scales are weighted in favor of one gender, or one race or one privileged background in a democracy, no one is very well served.

It is also true that women today have options their mothers and grandmothers never dreamed of having. Just 100 years ago we got the right to vote, and in the last century, we have witnessed incredible accomplishments from women leaders all over the world.

Women are natural leaders. We possess empathy, an orientation for teamwork and a commitment for getting the job done. We are servant leaders in the true sense of the word. We are dedicated, bright, talented and educated. We truly care about the world we live in, the company we work for and the circle of family and friends in our lives. We are inclusive in our leadership roles, and we give back to society. Our journey has been made easier because of the women who have gone before us. We all stand on the shoulders of those who have gone before us, and fly on the wings of eagles.

I encourage you, always, to seek the answer to the questions, "Who are You? What could you be?" The answer is yours alone, and the journey is your life story. Share your gift with others along the way and help make a difference in the world you live in!

Judy Woodruff

Judy Woodruff is CNN's prime anchor and senior correspondent. She anchors *Inside Politics with Judy Woodruff*, the nation's first program devoted exclusively to politics. She also co-anchors special coverage of political conventions and summits; she has reported on every national political convention and presidential campaign since 1976. From 1970-1974, she was a correspondent for WAGA-TV, the CBS affiliate in Atlanta, where she reported on the state legislature for five years and anchored the noon and evening news.

Woodruff has won a CableACE Award for Best Newscaster and a News and Documentary Emmy Award. She was the first recipient of the National Women's Hall of Fame President's 21st Century Award.

Woodruff is a founding co-chair of the International Women's Media Foundation, an organization dedicated to promoting and encouraging women in communication industries worldwide. Woodruff also serves on the board of trustees of the Freedom Forum, the Carnegie Corporation of New York and the Urban Institute. She and her husband, Al Hunt, were named "Washingtonians of the Year" by *Washingtonian* magazine for their fund-raising work to fight spina bifida.

THE VALUE OF THE VOTE
To the Atlanta-Fulton County League of Women Voters
Atlanta — February, 2001

I am here today to talk about this process that we all hold dear, this election process, and to talk about the value of voting, about the role of individuals in the electoral process, and the value of democracy itself. No one would disagree that these things are priceless. Nothing is more precious to us than our freedom, our right to choose our own leaders as we see fit, our right to vote.

You know, in reading a little bit about democracy, you find some interesting observations. Back in the 1940s, World War II was about to get under way. I found an anonymous quote, "Democracy is never won, but always to be won." Then in 1987, Marian Wright Edelman said, "Democracy is not a spectator sport," reflecting the concern at that time that too many people were sitting on the sidelines. And you may ask, how can anybody sit on the sidelines? Well, we can and we do.

We do in this country because most of us don't know what it's like not to live in a democracy. After all, women have had the right to vote since 1920, more than 80 years. On paper, blacks in this country have had the right to vote even longer. We all know that the voting reality for African Americans and other minorities in this country has not been nearly that simple, but the right has been there.

Look around the world. Today, human beings are the freest they have ever been in the history of our world. Almost six of every 10 people on earth now live in what we define as an electoral democracy. Four of those in countries that are truly considered free, such as the United States and the western European democracies, and the other two in countries partly free, with limited democratic rule and human rights protections. The other four of every 10 people on earth have no freedom or very little of it. But what a change from 100 years ago!

When the 20th Century began, no country was a democracy. No country on earth was a democracy with universal suffrage. In 1900, the United States, Britain and a few other countries came close, but we weren't there yet. Now, at the turn of the 21st Century, at least 120 of the world's 192 countries are functioning democracies.

And so many of us take our system of government for granted. And we take the right to vote for granted. Voter turnout in the United States — and that is the percentage of the voting-age population that actually goes to the poll on Election Day — has fallen from a high of 63 percent in 1960 when John Kennedy was running for president against Richard Nixon, to a pathetic 49 percent in 1996. Less than half the people who were eligible to vote went out and voted. This year, because you had a relatively interesting contest, turnout was up a whopping 2 percent. Officials can't give us a final number yet, but right now they've projected it would be at 51 percent, just barely more than at our lowest number ever.

> *So many of us take our system of government for granted. And we take the right to vote for granted.*

That's hardly something for us to be proud of.

And when you look even closer at the numbers, you find that turnout is lowest among the youngest eligible voters and among those with the least education. Not even one-third of young people aged 18 to 25 typically turn out to vote in presidential elections, whereas two-thirds of our senior citizens will show up at the polls. Between men and women, you will not be surprised to know, and I'm sure the League of Women Voters has something to do with this, women are slightly more likely to vote than men. And for many years, there have been more women voting in the United States than men. Individuals who did not finish high school vote in the smallest percentages. For people who went as far as the eighth grade, percentages are 20-30 percent. For people who finished high school, only 50 percent. If they went to college, 60 percent. If they went to graduate school, the percentages are in the 70s. In other words, it's directly related to how much education a person has.

Should we be satisfied with barely half of our total eligible electorate turning out? Hardly. All of these years we have been told until we were sick of hearing it, every vote counts. *Every vote counts* became the mantra that went in one ear and out the other for too many of us because we thought, "Well, they add it all up and if one person doesn't show up at the polls, it doesn't really matter." It became meaningless.

So on the night of Nov. 7, 2000, when we saw just how close the vote was in state after state after state — Wisconsin, Oregon, Iowa, New Mexico, Washington state, New Hampshire and, of course, Florida — we were jolted by that. The votes separating the winner from the loser sometimes were a few thousand and sometimes just a few hundred, out of millions of votes cast. We hadn't seen anything like it. If we ever believed that our votes didn't really matter, here, finally, was proof that they did.

I'm not going to rehash all the exciting events of the post-election process that played out over those 37 days. I'm sure it's just as embedded in your memory as it is in mine. But I do want to mention just a few of the highlights because I think they're important.

First, it was a very close election. Those 51 percent of Americans who went to the polls divided almost exactly evenly between George W. Bush and Al Gore. They each won 48 percent of the vote. Out of about 100 million ballots cast, Gore won the popular vote by about 500,000 votes. That is a margin of one-half of 1 percent of all the votes cast, in percentage terms one of the closest ever in the history of our country. You have to go back 120 years to find anything as close.

Still, we know, whatever we say about the popular vote, that's not what determines the outcome. It's the Electoral College vote. And any of us that might have forgotten that part of the Constitution were reminded of it vividly in this election.

The important lessons to emerge from Florida in my view were these: Every state in the country, not just Florida, needs a reliable, accurate, easy-to-access and easy-to-understand system of voting. In too many instances, that wasn't the case in Election 2000.

Second, far greater care needs to be taken to avoid irregularity. In Portland, Ore., they had a large number of people show up, unidentified, at the polling places and carry ballots away. They never figured out who they were.

Third, every vote counts. We may never have a presidential election as close as this one in our lifetime again. But we owe it to ourselves to make sure that the outcome reflects the wishes of the electorate. If people don't vote, that doesn't happen. If their votes are not reflected accurately, it doesn't happen.

> *Our credibility is our most important asset. If we lose that, it will be very difficult for us to win it back.*

Elections matter. Certainly who is the president matters because the decisions he makes every day affect our lives, whether it's the taxes we pay or the schools that we send our children to.

There are numerous efforts under way right now to improve our electoral system, and I would predict that the odds are pretty good that some form of electoral reform will pass this year.

I think all of us in the news media, and television in particular, have to answer for our premature and our wrong calls on election night — because I think that helped set the framework and the expectations for the election drama that played out in the days that followed.

It should be our role to encourage voter participation, to inform and nothing else. We have a role to play in this democracy. At the very least, we must take care not to mislead and certainly not to misinform. Our credibility is our most important asset. If we lose that, it will be very difficult for us to win it back. In my view, if we in the news media caused as much as one voter not to vote in the polls, then we let everyone down.

With that thought, I'm going to conclude my formal remarks and simply recall a remark by Winston Churchill. Someone asked him, "How do you describe democracy and the messy system that it often produces?" And he acknowledged, "It is the worst form of government on earth." But he added, "Except for all the others."

So we are very privileged to live in our democracy. Every vote does count!

Thank you.

EDITORIAL BOARD

JIM BARBER

Jim Barber oversees diversity communications and provides support to senior executives at Georgia Power. A former newspaper editor and reporter for United Press International and the *New York Daily News*, Barber graduated from the University of Georgia and lives in Gwinnett County with his wife, Becky, and three daughters, Dana, Tyler and Carrie.

TOMIKA DEPRIEST

Tomika DePriest is director of public relations for Spelman College. An award-winning communications professional, DePriest has also held editor posts at *Upscale Magazine, Atlanta Tribune* and Southern Company, and was producer of TurnerSouth.com.

MARY RATCLIFFE STYLES

Mary Ratcliffe Styles is an editorial consultant based in Atlanta. An honors graduate of the University of Georgia, her background includes corporate communications, public relations, magazine journalism and community newspaper management.

JEREMY WILSON

Jeremy Wilson was identified as one of Georgia's notable young writers in *O'Georgia: A Collection of Georgia's Newest and Most Promising Writers* in 1997. With an undergraduate degree from Georgia Tech and a graduate degree from Georgia State University, Jeremy currently works for a sports media firm in Chicago, where he lives with his wife and three cats.

WITH GRATEFUL APPRECIATION TO THE SPONSORS OF *ATLANTA WOMEN SPEAK*

Presenting Sponsor

Georgia Power, a unit of Southern Company, has been providing electricity to Georgia for more than a century. The company takes pride in its motto, "A Citizen Wherever We Serve" and its commitment to be a positive force in Georgia. Its employees play important roles in the communities they serve, volunteering for charities and service organizations, and supporting local community civic organizations. As the largest subsidiary of Southern Company, one of the nation's largest generators of electricity, Georgia Power is an investor-owned, tax-paying utility, with rates more than 15 percent below the national average. Georgia Power's 2 million customers are in all but six of Georgia's 159 counties.

Additional Sponsors

AGL Resources
The Atlanta Journal-Constitution
BEERS Skanska Inc.
The Coca-Cola Company
D. Clark Harris Inc.
Development Authority of Fulton County
Federal Home Loan Bank
Global Risk Managers
Heidelberg USA Inc.
MARTA
Meade Paper
MHR International
Montgomery Watson
Parsons Corporation

MaryAnne F. Gaunt
Audrey Hines
Mara Holley
Linda Jordan
Debbie McGinnis